EXPLORE THAILAND WITH PAUL (AND SANDY)

พิมพ์ครั้งแรก ธันวาคม พุทธศักราช 2567

ข้อมูลทางบรรณานุกรมของหอสมุดแห่งชาติ

Explore Thailand with Paul (and Sandy).- กรุงเทพฯ : Rabbit 4 Print, 2567.
228 หน้า.
1. ไทย-ภูมิประเทศและการท่องเที่ยว. 2. ไทย-ความเป็นอยู่และประเพณี.
I. ธรพร โถวรุ่งเรือง. II. สุกัญญา บุญจันทร์, ผู้วาดภาพประกอบ. III. ชื่อเรื่อง.

915.93
ISBN 978-616-619-209-4

คณะผู้จัดทำ

- ธรพร โถวรุ่งเรือง
- จีระภา ดีรักษา
- สุธีมา ศรีสำอางค์
- หทัยชนก เกิดกำบท

ศิลปกรรม : นางสาวสุกัญญา บุญจันทร์

จัดพิมพ์โดย : นางสาวธรพร โถวรุ่งเรือง

พิมพ์ที่ : Rabbit 4 Print 52/22 ซอยวิภาวดีรังสิต 66 แขวงตลาดบางเขน ตลาดบางเขน หลักสี่ กรุงเทพฯ 10210 โทรศัพท์ : 02-552-2222 Line : @Rabbit4printISBN

TSL4U

TSL4U

คำนำ

เอกสารประกอบการเรียนภาษาไทยสำหรับผู้ใหญ่ชาวต่างชาติชุดนี้จัดทำขึ้นโดยมีวัตถุประสงค์ที่จะช่วยให้ผู้เรียนสามารถนำไปใช้ประกอบการเรียนภาษาไทยได้อย่างสะดวก เข้าใจง่าย และช่วยพัฒนาศักยภาพในการเรียนรู้ภาษาไทยให้เป็นภาษาที่สองได้อย่างมีประสิทธิภาพ จนกระทั่งสามารถนำไปใช้สื่อสารกับผู้ที่ใช้ภาษาไทยในชีวิตประจำวันได้จริง

เอกสารประกอบการเรียนภาษาไทยชุดนี้ จัดทำขึ้นโดยอ้างอิงจากหลักสูตรการสอนภาษาไทยให้ชาวต่างชาติของ TSLTK (Thai as Second Language by Thai Kids Academy) ซึ่งเป็นสถาบันที่จดทะเบียนถูกต้องตามกฎหมายของประเทศออสเตรเลียตั้งแต่ปี พ.ศ. 2560

คณะผู้จัดทำหลักสูตร Thai Language Buddy by TSL4U Explore Thailand with Paul (and Sandy) ทุกคนเป็นคุณครูสอนภาษาไทยให้ชาวต่างชาติที่ผ่านการอบรมหลักสูตรการสอนภาษาไทยให้ชาวต่างชาติจากหลากหลายสถาบัน มีประสบการณ์ตรงในการสอนมามากกว่า 20 ปี และได้ร่วมกันพัฒนาหลักสูตรนี้ขึ้นมา ทั้งจากประสบการณ์การสอนจริงของคุณครูแต่ละท่าน และผลการตอบรับ (feedback) จากผู้เรียนภาษาไทยที่มาจากหลายประเทศทั่วโลก และมีระดับความรู้ความเข้าใจภาษาไทยที่แตกต่างกัน

เอกสารประกอบการเรียนภาษาไทยชุดนี้มุ่งหมายการจัดทำเนื้อหาให้ครอบคลุมการใช้ภาษาไทยในชีวิตประจำวันและสามารถนำไปใช้ได้ในสถานการณ์จริง ที่จะทำให้เอกสารฯ ชุดนี้เพื่อให้ตอบโจทย์ผู้เรียนให้ได้มากที่สุด

ทีมงาน TSLTK หวังเป็นอย่างยิ่งว่า เอกสารประกอบการเรียนภาษาไทยสำหรับผู้ใหญ่ชาวต่างชาติชุดนี้จะเป็นประโยชน์กับทั้งกับผู้เรียนและผู้ที่สนใจภาษาไทยทุกคน รวมถึงคุณครูผู้สอนภาษาไทยให้ชาวต่างชาติที่กำลังมองหาสื่อการสอนภาษาไทย และ (หรือ) ประกอบการสอนของตนได้อย่างมีประสิทธิภาพที่สุด

TSL4U

สารบัญ

บทที่ | หน้า

Chapter 1

ไม่เจอกันนานเลยและยินดีที่ได้รู้จัก

Mâi-jer-gan-naan-loiie láe yin-dee-têe-dâai-róo-jàk

Long time no see and nice to meet you.

ที่สนามบิน Têe sà-năam-bin

TSL4U

1
นี่น้องสาวของฉันชื่อสไมล์
Nêe nóng-săao kŏng chăn chêu Sà-mai
2
นี่พอลเพื่อนพี่ที่มหาวิทยาลัยที่ออสเตรเลีย
เขาย้ายมาทำงานที่เมืองไทย
Nêe Paul pêuuan pêe têe má-hăa-lai
têe Australia
Kăo yáai-maa-tam-ngaan têe-meuuang-tai

1
สวัสดีครับน้องสไมล์
ยินดีที่ได้รู้จักครับ
Sà-wàt-dee kráp nóng Sà-mai
Yin-dee-têe-dâai-róo-jàk kráp
2
ยินดีต้อนรับสู่ประเทศไทยค่ะ
Yin-dee-dtôn-ráp-sòo-bprà-têt-tai kâ

English Translation

At the airport.

Paul : Hi, Sandy. Long time no see. Thank you for picking me up.

Sandy : It's OK. Long time no see. How are you?

Paul : I am fine and very excited. How about you?

Sandy : I am fine too and also very happy to see you.

Sandy : This is my sister, named Smile. This is Paul, my friend from University in Australia. He moved to work in Thailand.

Paul : Hi, Smile. Nice to meet you.

Smile : Welcome to Thailand.

คำศัพท์ Vocabulary

Vocabulary	Definition	Note
 สนามบิน sà-năam bin	*Noun* airport	
กัน gan	*Personal Pronoun* one another, each other *Adverb* together, jointly	
นาน naan	*Adverb* for a long time	
เลย loiie	*Particle* We can't translate this meaning into a direct English equivalent. It adds emphasis and intensity to the meaning. It conveys a sense of "so much, completely, totally" in a positive sense, or "not at all, not even a little bit" in the negative sense.	
ก็เลย gôr-loiie	*None* as a result	
รับ ráp	*Verb* [to] receive, get, accept	
มารับ maa-ráp	*Verb* [to] come and get, pick up	

TSL4U

คำศัพท์ Vocabulary

Vocabulary	Definition	Note
แล้วก็ láew-gôr	*Conjunction* and then, and after that	
ด้วย dûuay	*Adverb* as well, also, too	
ได้ dâai	*SecondaryVerb* can, be able to	
สาว săao	*None* girl, young women	
 **น้องสาว** nóng-săao	*Noun* younger sister	
 **มหาวิทยาลัย** má-hăa-wít-tá-yaa-lai	*Noun* university	In spoken Thai, we often shorten the word and say มหาลัย (má-hăa- lai)

คำศัพท์ Vocabulary

Vocabulary	Definition	Note
 ออสเตรเลีย Australia	*Noun* Australia	
ย้าย yáai	*Verb* [to] move, transfer (from one location to another)	
ย้ายมา yáai-maa	*Verb* [to] move, transfer (from another place to this place)	
 เมือง meuuang	*None* city, town, state	
 เมืองไทย meuuang-tai	*None* Thailand	

Phrase

Phrase	Definition	Note
ไม่เจอกันนานเลย Mâi-jer-gan-naan-loiie	Long time no see.	
ยินดีต้อนรับ Yin-dee-dtôn-ráp	Welcome.	
ยินดีที่ได้รู้จัก Yin-dee-têe-dâai-róo-jàk	Nice to meet you.	
ยินดีต้อนรับสู่ประเทศไทย Yin-dee-dtôn-ráp-sòo-bprà-têt-tai	Welcome to Thailand.	

Exercise 1

Choose the correct sentence to complete the conversation.
เลือกประโยคที่ทำให้บทสนทนาสมบูรณ์

ที่มหาวิทยาลัย ประเทศออสเตรเลีย
Têe má-hăa-wít-tá-yaa-lai bprà-têt-Australia

 แสนดี: สวัสดีค่ะ ฉันชื่อแสนดี .... Săen-dee: Sà-wàt-dee kâ Chăn chêu Săen-dee ....  พอล: ยินดีที่ได้รู้จักเหมือนกันครับ ผมชื่อพอล Paul: Yin-dee-têe-dâai-róo-jàk mĕuuan-gan kráp Pŏm chêu Paul	1. ยินดีที่ได้รู้จักค่ะ Yin-dee-têe-dâai-róo-jàk kâ 2. ไม่เจอกันนานเลยค่ะ Mâi-jer-gan-naan-loiie kâ

 พอล: ผมเป็นคนออสเตรเลีย แล้วคุณล่ะ Paul: Pŏm bpen kon-Australia Láew-kun-lâ  แสนดี: .... Săen-dee:	1. ฉันเป็นคนไทยค่ะ Chăn bpen kon-tai kâ 2. น้องสาวของฉันชื่อสไมล์ค่ะ Nóng-săao kŏng chăn chêu Sà-mai kâ

พอล: ผมเคยไปเที่ยวประเทศไทย แล้วก็อยากไปทำงานที่นั่นด้วย Paul: Pǒm koiie bpai-tîieow bprà-têt-tai. láew-gôr yàak bpai tam-ngaan têe-nân dûuay. แสนดี: ฉันชอบที่นี่ .... Sǎen-dee: Chǎn chôp têe-nêe	1. นี่คือเพื่อนของคุณใช่ไหม Nêe-keu pêuuan-kǒng-kun châi- mái 2. อยากย้ายมาอยู่เลย Yàak yáai-maa-yòo loiie

พอล: คุณอยู่ที่ออสเตรเลียนานหรือยังครับ Paul: Kun yòo-têe Australia naan réu-yang kráp แสนดี: .... ฉันยังตื่นเต้นอยู่เลย Sǎen-dee: .... Chǎn yang dtèun-dtên yòo loiie	1. ไม่นานค่ะ Mâi-naan kâ 2. มหาวิทยาลัยที่เมืองไทยเรียน 4 ปีค่ะ Má-hǎa-wít-tá-yaa-lai têe meuuang-tai riian sèe bpee kâ

พอล: ยินดีต้อนรับสู่ประเทศออสเตรเลียครับ Paul: Yin-dee-dtôn-ráp-sòo-bprà-têt-Australia kráp แสนดี: .... Sǎen-dee:	1. คุณมารับฉันได้ไหมคะ Kun maa-ráp chǎn dâai-mái ká 2. ขอบคุณค่ะ Kòp-kun kâ

“

Exercise 2 Make sentences using these words.
แต่งประโยคจากคำที่กำหนด

1.) ของ (kŏng)

....

2.) นาน (naan)

....

3.) มารับ (maa-ráp)

....

4.) ดีใจ (dee-jai) เจอ (jer)

....

5.) ด้วยกัน (dûuay-gan) เมืองไทย (meuuang-tai)

....

Grammar 1

นี่น้องสาวของฉัน
Nêe nóng-săao kŏng chăn
This is my younger sister.

Structure: นี่ (nêe) + someone or something + ของ (kŏng) + person

Explanation: It is used to introduce or specify someone or something's ownership.

Example:

Statement: นี่ขนมของคุณ
Nêe kà-nŏm kŏng kun
This is your sweet.

Negation: นี่ไม่ใช่ขนมของผม
Nêe mâi-châi kà-nŏm kŏng pŏm
This is not my sweet.

Closed question: นี่ขนมของคุณใช่มั้ย
Nêe kà-nŏm kŏng kun châi-mái
Is this your sweet?

Opened question: นี่ขนมของใคร
Nêe kà-nŏm kŏng krai
Whose sweet is this?

Exercise 1

Read Thai sentences and translate them into English.
อ่านประโยคภาษาไทยและแปลเป็นภาษาอังกฤษ

1.) นี่สัตว์เลี้ยงของเขา
Nêe sàt-líiang kǒng kǎo

....

2.) นี่ไม่ใช่สัตว์เลี้ยงของเธอ
Nêe mâi-châi sàt-líiang kǒng ter

....

3.) นี่สัตว์เลี้ยงของพวกเราใช่มั้ย
Nêe sàt-líiang kǒng pûuak-rao châi-mái

....

4.) นี่สัตว์เลี้ยงของใคร
Nêe sàt-líiang kǒng krai

....

5.) นั่นสัตว์เลี้ยงของใคร
Nân sàt-líiang kǒng krai

....

Exercise 2

Say these sentences in Thai.
พูดประโยคต่อไปนี้เป็นภาษาไทย

1. This is my book.
2. This isn't your book.
3. Is this your book?
4. Whose book is this?
5. Whose book is that?

Grammar 2

☞เพื่อนพี่

Pêuuan pêe

My friend.

(It is literally translated as the friend of bigger brother or bigger sister. However, Thai people can address themselves according to their relative role. So 'pêe' in this sentence is referring to the speaker Sandy in replacement of the personal pronoun "I"; and "pêuuan pêe" here means 'my friend' for the speaker Sandy.

Structure: someone or something + someone

Explanation: in Thai, we can omit the word "ของ" (kǒng) in most cases and the phrases still have the same meanings.

Example:

- เพื่อนพี่ (pêuuan pêe) is the same as เพื่อนของพี่ (pêuuan kǒng pêe)
  My friend (the friend of bigger brother or bigger sister.)

- แฟนผม (faen pǒm) is the same as แฟนของผม (faen kǒng pǒm)
  My partner (for male).

- บ้านครู (bâan kroo) is the same as บ้านของครู (bâan kǒng kroo)
  Teacher's house

- ก๋วยเตี๋ยวใคร (gǔuay-dtǐieow krai) is the same as
  ก๋วยเตี๋ยวของใคร (gǔuay-dtǐieow kǒng krai)
  Whose noodles ?

Exercise 1

Read Thai sentences and translate them into English.
อ่านประโยคภาษาไทยและแปลเป็นภาษาอังกฤษ

1.) ภรรยาเขา
Pan-rá-yaa kăo

....

2.) สามีฉัน
Săa-mee chăn

....

3.) ห้องนอนผม
Hông-non pŏm

....

4.) ที่ทำงานใคร
Têe-tam-ngaan krai

....

5.) ที่ทำงานคุณใช่มั้ย
Têe-tam-ngaan kun châi-mái

....

Exercise 2

Say these phrases in Thai.
พูดวลีต่อไปนี้เป็นภาษาไทย

1. Your country.
2. Your rice.
3. My hotel.
4. Whose car?
5. Whose motorbike?

Grammar 3

☞แล้วคุณล่ะ

Láew-kun-lâ

What about you?

Structure: แล้ว (láew) + someone or something + ล่ะ (lâ)

Explanation: we use this structure to ask the same question as the previous one with a different object or person. This is equivalent to English way of asking "what about ...?" or "How about ...?"

Example:

1. แล้วพ่อล่ะ
   Láew-pôr-lâ
   How about dad?

2. แล้วแฟนคุณล่ะ
   Láew-faen-kun-lâ
   What about your partner?

3. แล้วแฟนของคุณล่ะ
   Láew-faen-kŏng-kun-lâ
   What about your partner?

4. แล้วที่ทำงานของคุณล่ะ
   Láew-têe-tam-ngaan-kŎng-kun-lâ
   What about your workplace?

5. แล้วพรุ่งนี้ล่ะ
   Láew-prûng-née-lâ
   What about tomorrow?

Exercise 1

Read Thai sentences and translate them into English.
อ่านประโยคภาษาไทยและแปลเป็นภาษาอังกฤษ

1.) ฉันสบายดี แล้วคุณล่ะ
Chăn sà-baai-dee Láew-kun-lâ

....

2.) พี่ไปร้านค้า แล้วแม่ล่ะ
Pêe bpai ráan-káa Láew-mâe-lâ

....

3.) ขนมอร่อย แล้วกาแฟล่ะ
Kà-nŏm à-ròi Láew-gaa-fae-lâ

....

4.) วันนี้เขาไม่มา แล้วพรุ่งนี้ล่ะ
Wan-née kăo mâi maa Láew-prûng-née-lâ

....

5.) ที่นี่ฝนตก แล้วที่นั่นล่ะ
Têe-nêe fŏn-dtòk Láew-têe-nân-lâ

....

Exercise 2

Say these sentences in Thai.
พูดประโยคต่อไปนี้เป็นภาษาไทย

1. I like sports. What about you?
2. My clothes are wet. What about yours?
3. The hat is expensive. What about the glasses?
4. Thailand is very hot. What about your country?
5. Tom-yum is spicy and sour. What about Som-tum?

Fun Fact: Thai names.

Most Thai people have an official name and a nickname. Official names often have first name and last name only. Very few people have middle name. Thai nicknames are what we are commonly known for. For some friends and colleagues, we do not even know their official name. In this story, Sandy and Smile are their nicknames.

Challenge: Say these sentences in Thai.
พูดประโยคต่อไปนี้เป็นภาษาไทย

1. Paul and Sandy are friends from a university in Australia.
2. Paul moved to Thailand to work.
3. Sandy and Smile came and picked him up at the airport.

Chapter 2

ไปอโศกยังไง

Bpai-à-sòhk-yang-ngai

How to go to Asok?

ที่คอนโด Têe kon-doh

ที่สถานี BTS อโศก Têe sà-tăa-nee BTS à-sòhk

English Translation

At Paul's apartment

Paul	:	Excuse me, how to get from here to Asok?
Building manager	:	You can go by taxi, motorcycle taxi, and BTS. Which way would you take?
Paul	:	I have to go to work every day. Which way do you think I should take?
Building manager	:	I think you should take the BTS. Walk out to the left. When you reach 7-11, then turn right. Walk straight for about 500 meters. And then you will arrive at On-Nut station.

At Asok Station

Paul	:	Excuse me, how to get from here to the A Tower?
Taxi rider	:	You can walk along the main street. It takes about a kilometer and a half.
Paul	:	If I go with you, how much does it cost?
Taxi rider	:	15 baht. Do you want to go?
Paul	:	Yes, I do.

TSL4U

คำศัพท์ Vocabulary

Vocabulary	Definition	Note
 คอนโด kon-doh	*Noun* condo	
นะ ná	*Particle* We can't translate this meaning into a direct English equivalent. It's a particle used to make a sentence seem softer, more persuasive or less abrupt.	
ยังไง Yang-ngai	*Interrogative* 1. how, what *Adverb* 2. in any way, whichever way	
ทั้ง táng	*PreposedAdjective* all, entire, whole	
 แท็กซี่ Taxi	*Noun* Taxi; cab	
 วินมอเตอร์ไซค์ win-mor-dter-sai	*Noun* motorcycle taxi	

TSL4U

คำศัพท์ Vocabulary

Vocabulary	Definition	Note
 BTS BTS	*Noun* Bangkok Transit System	MRT (Metropolitan Rapid Transit)
ทาง taang	*Noun; Classifier* 1. way, path, route *Preposition* 2. by	
ทางไหน taang-nǎi	*Interrogative* which way?	
 ทางซ้าย taang-sáai	*Noun* left side	
ทุก túk	*Quantifier* every, each	
ทุกวัน túk-wan	*Adverb* every day, always, all the times	

คำศัพท์ Vocabulary

Vocabulary	Definition	Note
ดีกว่า dee-gwàa	*Stative Verb, Comparative Adjective* [to be] better	
พอ por	*Conjunction* 1. as soon as, when, just when, just after *Stative Verb, Adjective* 2. [to be] enough, sufficient, appropriate	
เลี้ยว líieow	*Verb* [to] turn	
 **ตรง** dtrong	*Verb* 1. [to] be in accordance (with), be consistent (with) 2. [to] be precise at, be exact, be accurate *Stative Verb, Adjective* 3. [to be] straight, direct *Preposition* 4. at	
อีก èek	*Adverb* again, once more, more	
ประมาณ bprà-maan	*Adverb* 1. about, around, approximately *Verb* 2. [to] estimate, approximate, reckon	

TSL4U

คำศัพท์ Vocabulary

Vocabulary	Definition	Note
 ตึก dtèuk	*Noun* building, tower	
ตาม dtaam	*Preposition* 1. along, around, among, through *Verb* 2. [to] follow, pursue, come after *Preposition* 3. according to, in accordance with	
เดินตาม dern-dtaam	*Combined verb* [to] walk behind, follow	
 ถนน tà-nŏn	*Noun* road, street, avenue	
ถนนใหญ่ tà-nŏn-yài	*Combined noun* main street	
กิโล gì-loh	*Noun* 1. weight scale 2. kilogram 3.kilometer	
ครึ่ง krêung	*Noun* half	
กิโลครึ่ง gì-loh-krêung	*Combined noun* 1. one and a half kilometer 2. one and a half kilogram	

Exercise 1 Look at the picture and complete the conversation.
ดูรูปภาพและเติมประโยคต่อไปนี้ให้สมบูรณ์

1. A: ขอโทษนะคะ ไป Sandy's Coffee Shop เท่าไหร่คะ
Kŏr-tôht ná-ká Bpai Sandy's Coffee Shop tâo-rài ká

B: ....

2. A: ....

B: ราคาตามมิเตอร์เลยครับ
Raa-kaa-dtaam-mí-dtêr-loiie kráp

3. A: ขอบคุณที่มารับนะ รอนานมั้ย
Kòp-kun-têe-maa-ráp ná Ror-naan-mái

B: ....

Exercise 2

Put these words in the correct order.
เรียงคำให้เป็นประโยคที่ถูกต้อง

1.) จาก ยังไง ที่นี่ ไป สนามบิน
jàak yang-ngai têe-nêe bpai sà-năam-bin

2.) ไป เท่าไหร่ ราคา โรงพยาบาล
bpai tâo-rài raa-kaa rohng-pá-yaa-baan

3.) ผม ทุกวัน เดิน ทำงาน ไป
pŏm túk-wan dern tam-ngaan bpai

4.) สถานีรถไฟ แท็กซี่ ไป ราคา 65 บาท
sà-tăa-nee-rót-fai Taxi bpai raa-kaa hòk-sìp-hâa bàat

5.) ถึง เลี้ยว ขวา ตลาด แล้ว
tĕung líieow kwăa dtà-làat láew

Grammar 1

ไปทางไหนดี

Bpai-taang-năi-dee

Which way should (I) go?

Structure: opened question + ดี (dee)

Explanation: ดี (dee) on its own means good. ดี (dee) at the end of opened question can be indirectly translated as 'should'. This structure is very common in spoken Thai.

Example:

1. วันนี้กินอะไรดี
   Wan-née gin-à-rai-dee
   What should (we) eat today?

2. พรุ่งนี้ไปที่ไหนดี
   Prûng-née bpai-têe-năi-dee
   Where should (we) go tomorrow?

3. ดูหนังกับใครดี
   Doo-năng-gàp-krai-dee
   Whom should (I) watch the movie with?

4. ไปหาแม่เมื่อไหร่ดี
   Bpai-hăa-mâe-mêuua-rài-dee
   When should (I) visit mum?

5. บอกเขายังไงดี
   Bòk-kăo-yang-ngai-dee
   How should (I) tell him?

Exercise 1

Read Thai sentences and translate them into English.
อ่านประโยคภาษาไทยและแปลเป็นภาษาอังกฤษ

1.) เจอกันกี่โมงดี
Jer-gan gèe-mohng-dee

....

2.) พวกเราไปตลาดน้ำเมื่อไหร่ดี
Pûuak-rao bpai dtà-làat-náam mêuua-rài-dee

....

3.) ผมเรียนภาษาไทยที่ไหนดี
Pŏm riian paa-săa-tai têe-năi-dee

....

4.) เย็นนี้เราจะกินอะไรดี
Yen-née rao jà-gin à-rai-dee

....

5.) คุณคิดว่าฉันใส่ชุดไหนดี
Kun kít-wâa chăn sài chút-năi-dee

....

Exercise 2

Say these sentences in Thai.
พูดประโยคต่อไปนี้เป็นภาษาไทย

1. What should we drink tonight?
2. Whom should I ask?
3. Where should I go to travel?
4. How should I go?
5. Which way should I go?

Grammar 2

พอเจอ 7-11 ก็เลี้ยวขวา

Por jer seven-eleven gôr líieow kwăa

When (you) reach 7-11, then turn right.

Structure: พอ (por) + sentence + (subject) + ก็ (gôr) + sentence

Explanation: พอ (por) by itself means 'as soon as' or 'to be enough'. ก็ (gôr) by itself means 'also, then or therefore'. The structure 'พอ (por) ...... ก็ (gôr) ......' is to combine 2 sentences together to indicate that sentence 1 is immediately followed by sentence 2; in the same way as structure 'when .... then......' in English.

Example:

1. พออยู่เมืองไทยนาน ๆ ก็ทำอาหารไทยได้
   Por yòo meuuang-tai naan-naan gôr tam aa-hăan-tai dâai
   When stay in Thailand for a long time, can cook Thai food.

2. พอกินข้าวแล้ว ก็กินยา
   Por gin kâao láew gôr gin yaa
   As soon as finish eating, then take medicine.

3. พอเขามา เธอก็ไป
   Por kăo maa ter gôr bpai
   As soon as he comes, she goes.

Exercise 1

Read Thai sentences and translate them into English.
อ่านประโยคภาษาไทยและแปลเป็นภาษาอังกฤษ

1.) พอไม่กินข้าว ก็ปวดท้อง
Por mâi-gin kâao gôr bpùuat-tóng

....

2.) พอฉันรู้จักเขา ฉันก็ชอบเขา
Por chăn róo-jàk kăo chăn gôr chôp kăo

....

3.) พอฉันพูด คุณก็ไม่ฟัง
Por chăn pôot kun gôr mâi-fang

....

4.) พอไม่เจอเพื่อนนาน ๆ ฉันก็เหงา
Por mâi-jer pêuuan naan-naan chăn gôr ngăo

....

5.) พอวันหยุด ใคร ๆ ก็อยากไปเที่ยว
Por wan-yùt krai-krai gôr yàak-bpai-tîieow

....

Exercise 2

Say these sentences in Thai.
พูดประโยคต่อไปนี้เป็นภาษาไทย

1. When it rains, the clothes are wet.
2. When I am full, I want to sleep.
3. When you see 7-11, go straight for one and a half kilometer.
4. When mum is not home, the little brother is plays game.
5. When the car is old, the price is cheaper.

Grammar 3

เดินตรงไปอีกประมาณ 500 เมตร แล้วก็จะเจอสถานี BTS อ่อนนุช
Dern-dtrong-bpai èek bprà-maan hâa-rói-mét
Láew-gôr jà jer sà-tăa-nee-BTS-òn-nút
Walk straight for about 500 meters. And then you will arrive at On-nut station.

Structure: sentence + แล้วก็ (láew-gôr) + sentence

Explanation: แล้ว (láew) by itself means 'already' often found at the end of sentence to indicate its experience. ก็ (gôr) by itself means 'also' or 'then' usually placed after subject at the beginning of sentences. When combining the two together, แล้วก็ (láew-gôr) means 'and then' or 'and after that'.

Example:

1. ฉันชอบสีขาว สีแดง แล้วก็สีน้ำเงิน
Chăn chôp sěe-kăao sěe-daeng láew-gôr sěe-náam-ngern
I like white, red and (then) blue.

2. เขาอยากไปกรุงเทพ เชียงใหม่ กระบี่ แล้วก็ภูเก็ต
Kăo yàak bpai grung-têp chiiang-mài grà-bèe láew-gôr poo-gèt
He wants to go to Bangkok, Chiangmai, Krabi and (then) Phuket.

3. มาถึงที่ร้านอาหาร แล้วก็เข้ามาได้เลย
Maa-těung têe-ráan-aa-hăan láew-gôr kâo-maa-dâai-loiie
When (you) arrive at the restaurant, (and) then (you) can come in.

4. เราเจอกันที่สถานี BTS แล้วก็เดินไปด้วยกันดีไหม
Rao jer-gan têe-sà-tăa-nee-BTS láew-gôr dern-bpai-dûuay-gan dee-măi
We meet at BTS station and then walk together, is this good?

Exercise 1

Read Thai sentences and translate them into English.
อ่านประโยคภาษาไทยและแปลเป็นภาษาอังกฤษ

1.) ฉันไม่ชอบสีเหลือง สีเขียว แล้วก็สีน้ำเงิน
Chăn mâi-chôp sěe-lěuuang sěe-kiieow láew-gôr sěe-náam-ngern

....

2.) เธออยากไปปารีส นิวยอร์ก ดูไบ แล้วก็ซิดนีย์
Ter yàak-bpai Paris New york Dubai láew-gôr Sydney

....

3.) ไปถึงสนามบิน แล้วก็เช็กอินได้เลย
Bpai-těung sà-năam-bin láew-gôr check-in dâai-loiie

....

4.) ฉันไม่เจอเธอนาน แล้วก็ไม่มีเบอร์เธอด้วย
Chăn mâi jer ter naan láew-gôr mâi-mee ber-ter dûuay

....

5.) พอถึง 7-11 แล้วก็เลี้ยวซ้ายใช่มั้ย
Por těung seven-eleven láew-gôr líieow-sáai châi-mái

....

Exercise 2

Say these sentences in Thai.
พูดประโยคต่อไปนี้เป็นภาษาไทย

1. I want fried rice, Tom-yum and then spicy curry chicken.
2. She orders Som-tum, green curry beef, and then what else?
3. Go to eat, and then go shopping.
4. I do not like chocolate, and then do not eat chocolate.
5. Study Thai on Tuesday, Wednesday and then Thursday.

Fun Fact: Thai people rarely travel on foot.

In Thailand, most people do not prefer walking because of the hot weather and the often unfavourable street conditions for pedestrians (such as stray dogs, street vendors, and sometimes even motorcycles riding on the foodpaths). Thai people tend to travel using vehicles, even for short distances. This is one of the reasons why there are many motorcycle taxis available in various locations, especially near the train stations like the MRT and the BTS.

Challenge: Say these sentences in Thai.
พูดประโยคต่อไปนี้เป็นภาษาไทย

1. Paul's apartment is at On-nut station.
2. Paul has to go to work at Asok station every day.
3. Paul takes motorcycle taxi from Asok station to work for 15 Baht.

Chapter 3

ผมพูดไทยได้นิดหน่อย

Pŏm pôot-tai-dâai-nít-nòi

I can speak Thai a little bit.

ที่ร้านกาแฟ Têe ráan gaa-fae

1
รับอะไรดีคะ
Ráp-à-rai-dee ká
2
เอาชาไทยเย็นไม่หวาน 1 แก้ว
ขอน้ำแข็งเยอะ ๆ ด้วยครับ
Ao chaa-tai-yen mâi-wăan nèung-gâew
Kŏr náam-kăeng yúh-yúh dûuay kráp
3
รับเป็นแก้วอะไรดีคะ เล็ก กลาง หรือใหญ่
Ráp-bpen-gâew-à-rai-dee ká
Lék glaang rĕu yài
4
แก้วเล็กก็พอครับ
Gâew-lék-gôr-por kráp

1
เท่าไหร่ครับ
Tâo-rài kráp
2
30 บาทค่ะ
Săam-sìp-bàat kâ
3
ผมใช้บัตรเครดิตได้มั้ย
Pŏm chái bàt-kray-dìt
dâai-mái
4
อุ๊ย! ร้านเราไม่รับบัตรเครดิตค่ะ
รับแต่เงินสดกับสแกน QR Code ค่ะ
Úi! Ráan-rao mâi-ráp bàt-kray-dìt kâ
Ráp dtàe ngern-sòt gàp
scan QR code kâ
5
งั้นผมสแกนจ่ายแล้วกันครับ
Ngán pŏm scan-jàai
-láew-gan kráp

English Translation

At the coffee shop

Paul : Can you speak English?

Seller : Yes, I can but not very well.

Paul : No problem.
I can speak Thai a little.

Paul : I have learnt Thai language for 2 years already.
: I like Thailand very much.

Seller : Oh! You speak Thai so clearly.
Seller : Can speak like this, not a little at all

Seller : What would you like to get?

Paul : I want a glass of unsweetened iced Thai Tea and can I have I lot of ice as well, please

Seller : Which (size of) glass would you like to get: small medium or large?

Paul : A small one is enough.

Paul : How much is it?

Seller : It's 30 baht.

Paul : Can I use credit card?

Seller : Oh! Our store doesn't accept credit cards. We only take cash and QR code.

Paul : I'll scan to pay then.

คำศัพท์ Vocabulary

Vocabulary	Definition	Note
 อังกฤษ ang-grìt	*Noun* 1. England, Britain *Adjective* 2. English	
 เก่ง gèng	*Particle* 1. excellently; expertly; proficiently *StativeVerb ; Adjective* 2. [to be] skilled; talented; proficient	
 นิดหน่อย nít-nòi	*Adverb* a little bit; just a little; a tiny bit	
โอ้โห ôh-hŏh	*Interjection* It's an interjection showing surprise, admiration or amazement at something.	
ชัด chát	*Adverb* 1. clearly; obviously; explicitly *StativeVerb ; Adjective* 2. [to be] clear; sharp; distinct	
แบบ bàep	*Noun ; Classifier* 1. model; style; way *Adverb* 2. like; as; in the same way as	
 ชาไทย chaa-tai	*Noun* Thai tea	

คำศัพท์ Vocabulary

Vocabulary	Definition	Note
ขอ kŏr	*Verb* [to] ask for; request for; ask	
 **น้ำแข็ง** náam-kăeng	*Noun* ice	
เยอะ yúh	*Adverb* much	
 **กลาง** glaang	*Noun* 1. center; middle *StativeVerb; Adjective* 2. [to be] central; medium	
ก็พอ gôr-por	*Combined words* That's enough.	
ใช้ chái	*Verb* [to] use	

คำศัพท์ Vocabulary

Vocabulary	Definition	Note
 บัตรเครดิต bàt-kray-dìt	*Noun* credit card	
อุ๊ย úi	*Interjection* oh!; oops!	
ร้าน ráan	*Noun* shop; store; booth	
แต่ dtàe	*Adverb* 1. only; just *Conjunction* 2. but *Preposition* 3. from; since	
 เงิน ngern	*Noun* 1. money; currency; cash 2. silver	
สด sòt	*Adverb* 1. live *StativeVerb; Adjective* 2. [to be] fresh	

คำศัพท์ Vocabulary

Vocabulary	Definition	Note
 เงินสด ngern-sòt	*Noun* cash	
สแกน scan	*Verb* scan	
QR Code QR code	*Noun* QR Code	
งั้น ngán	*Adverb* 1. like that *Conjunction* 2. if so; in that case; then	
จ่าย jàai	*Verb* 1. [to] pay; spend *Verb* 2. [to] distribute; disburse; divide	
แล้วกัน láew gan	*Adverb* then	

Exercise 1 Listen to Thai sentences from your teacher and select the picture according to the sentence.

ฟังคุณครูพูดภาษาไทยและเลือกรูปภาพที่สอดคล้องกับประโยคที่คุณครูพูด

1. ผมไม่เคยเรียนภาษาไทย ผมพูดภาษาไทยไม่ได้เลย

A.

B.

C.

2. ฉันเรียนภาษาไทยมา 3 ปีแล้ว

A.

B.

C.

3. ขอกาแฟร้อนแก้วเล็ก 1 แก้ว

A.

B.

C.

4. ราคา ๕๕ บาท

A.

B.

C.

5. ร้านนี้รับบัตรเครดิต

A.

B.

C.

Exercise 2

Complete sentences with correct words.
เติมคำในช่องว่างด้วยคำที่ถูกต้อง

นิดหน่อย nít-nòi	ได้มั้ย dâai-mái	QR Code QR code	1 แก้ว nèung-gâew	ไม่รับ mâi-ráp

1. ผมนั่งวินมอเตอร์ไซค์ไปบ้านคุณ ....

   Pŏm nâng win-mor-dtêr-sai bpai bâan kun ....

2. ผมขอสแกน ....ครับ

   Pŏm kŏr scan .... kráp

3. เอาส้มตำใส่พริก ....

   Ao sôm-dtam sài-prík ....

4. ที่นี่ .... บัตรเครดิตค่ะ

   Têe-nêe .... bàt-kray-dìt kâ

5. เอาโค้ก .... ใส่น้ำแข็งนิดหน่อย

   Ao coke .... sài-náam-kăeng nít-nòi

Grammar 1

คุณพูดภาษาอังกฤษได้มั้ย

Kun pôot paa-săa ang-grìt dâai mái

Can you speak English?

Structure:

- Statement: subject + verb (+ extension*) + ได้ (dâai)
- Negative sentence: subject + verb (+ extension*) + ไม่ได้ (mâi-dâai)
- Question: subject + verb (+ extension*) + ได้มั้ย (dâai-mái)
- Note: extension* can be secondary verb, noun, or adverb

Explanation: ได้ (dâai) in Thai has 3 meanings: (1) to get or to receive eg. ได้เงิน (dâai ngern) to receive money. (2) a helping verb showing ability eg. พูดได้ (pôot-dâai) can speak. (3) a helping verb making the main verb become past tense eg. ได้กิน (dâai-gin) to have eaten.

Although ได้ (dâai) is widely used in Thai; one of the most common uses is referring to someone's ability to do something as mentioned in structures explanation 2.

Example:

- Statement: ผมพูดภาษาไทยได้ (Pŏm-pôot paa-săa-tai dâai)
  I can speak Thai language.
- Negative sentence: ผมพูดภาษาไทยไม่ได้ (Pŏm pôot paa-săa-tai mâi-dâai)
  I can't speak Thai language.
- Question: คุณพูดภาษาไทยได้มั้ย (Kun pôot paa-săa-tai dâai-mái)
  Can you speak Thai language?

Exercise 1

Read Thai sentences and translate them into English.
อ่านประโยคภาษาไทยและแปลเป็นภาษาอังกฤษ

1.) ฉันทำต้มยำกุ้งได้
Chăn tam dtôm-yam-gûng dâai

....

2.) คุณพูดช้า ๆ ได้มั้ย
Kun pôot-cháa-cháa dâai-mái

....

3.) ผมไปไม่ได้
Pŏm bpai mâi-dâai

....

4.) คุณเล่นไอซ์สเก็ตได้มั้ย
Kun lên ice-skate dâai-mái

....

5.) ฉันนั่งที่ไหนได้
Chăn nâng têe-năi dâai

....

Exercise 2

Say these sentences in Thai.
พูดประโยคต่อไปนี้เป็นภาษาไทย

1. I cannot go with you.
2. I can cook Pad Thai.
3. What can you cook?
4. Can you walk slowly?
5. Can I drive in Thailand?

Grammar 2

ผมเรียนภาษาไทยมา 2 ปีแล้ว

Pŏm riian paa-săa-tai maa sŏng bpee láew

I have learnt Thai language for 2 years already.

Structure: subject + verb (+ extension) + มา (maa) + period of time + แล้ว (láew)

Explanation: มา (maa) on its own means 'to come' but it is also used to indicate 'past tense' or 'present perfect' tenses. As Thai verbs do not conjugate to reflect tenses; we put additional words (can be in front, middle or at the end of sentences). มา (maa) in the structure 'มา (ma) + period of time + แล้ว (láew)' is used to indicate something has started in the past and still effecting until now; which is equivalent to 'present perfect tense' in English.

Example:

1. ผมรอคุณมา 30 นาทีแล้ว
   Pŏm ror kun maa săam-sìp-naa-tee láew
   I have waited for you for 30 minutes already.

2. รูมเมทของฉันไม่อาบน้ำมา 3 วันแล้ว
   Roommate-kŏng-chăn mâi-àap-náam maa săam-wan láew
   My roommate hasn't had a shower for 3 days already.

3. รูมเมทคุณไม่อาบน้ำมา 3 วันแล้วเหรอ
   Roommate-kun mâi-àap-náam maa săam-wan láew rĕr
   Your roommate hasn't had a shower for 3 days already, has she/he?

4. เขาอยู่เมืองไทยมากี่ปีแล้ว
   Kăo yòo meuuang-tai maa gèe-bpee láew
   How many years has he lived in Thailand?

Exercise 1

Read Thai sentences and translate them into English.
อ่านประโยคภาษาไทยและแปลเป็นภาษาอังกฤษ

1.) ฉันทำงานที่นี่มา 6 ปีแล้ว
Chăn tam-ngaan têe-nêe maa hòk-bpee láew

....

2.) ผมทำงานนี้มา 5 วันแล้ว
Pŏm tam-ngaan née maa hâa-wan láew

....

3.) เขาหยุดงานมากี่วันแล้ว
Kăo yùt-ngaan maa gèe-wan láew

....

4.) เขาไม่ทำงานมากี่วันแล้ว
Kăo mâi-tam-ngaan maa gèe-wan láew

....

5.) เขาไม่ทำงานมา 2 สัปดาห์แล้วเหรอ
Kăo mâi tam-ngaan maa sŏng-sàp-daa láew rĕr

....

Exercise 2

Say these sentences in Thai.
พูดประโยคต่อไปนี้เป็นภาษาไทย

1. Little brother has played game for 3 hours already.
2. How many days has it rained?
3. How many months have you learnt Thai?
4. My pet has not eaten food for 2 days already.
5. Your pet has not eaten food for 2 days already, is it true?

Grammar 3

ขอน้ำแข็งเยอะ ๆ

Kŏr-náam-kăeng-yúh-yúh

Request a lot of ice (Please give me a lot of ice.)

Structure: word + repeated word

Explanation: in Thai, we repeat a word twice to emphasize or exaggerate its meaning. For example, ดี (dee) by itself means 'good'; if you say ดี ๆ (dee-dee), it would mean 'very good'. Sometimes, repeated word can also be used to make the root word plural. For example, เด็ก (dèk) means 'child' and เด็ก ๆ (dèk- dèk) means children. Rarely, repeated word can also to form a new word. For example, งู ๆ ปลา ๆ (ngoo-ngoo-bplaa-bplaa) does not have anything to do with snake or fish; but it means 'a little bit' – when referring to skills.

Note: in Thai script, the repeated word is written with 'ๆ' (mái-yá-mók) symbol.

Example:

1. เขียนสวย ๆ
   Kĭian sŭuay-sŭuay
   Write beautifully.

2. พูดตรง ๆ
   Pôot dtrong-dtrong
   Speak honestly.

3. เพื่อน ๆ อยู่ที่ไหน
   Pêuuan-pêuuan yòo-têe-năi
   Where are (your) friends?

4. เด็ก ๆ เล่นที่หน้าบ้าน
   Dèk-dèk lên têe nâa-bâan
   Children play in front of the house.

5. ไป ๆ มา ๆ พวกเราก็เป็นเพื่อนกัน
   Bpai-bpai-maa-maa pûuak-rao gôr bpen pêuuan gan
   Eventually, we are friends.

Exercise 1

Read Thai sentences and translate them into English.
อ่านประโยคภาษาไทยและแปลเป็นภาษาอังกฤษ

1.) นั่งดี ๆ
Nâng dee-dee

....

2.) ขอผลไม้ชิ้นเล็ก ๆ
Kŏr pŏn-lá-mái chín lék-lék

....

3.) ฉันพูดภาษาไทยได้งู ๆ ปลา ๆ
Chăn pôot paa-săa-tai dâai ngoo-ngoo-bplaa-bplaa

....

4.) แม่ทำอะไร ๆ ก็อร่อย
Mâe tam à-rai-à-rai gôr à-ròi

....

5.) ไหน ๆ เธอก็อยู่ที่นี่แล้ว
Năi-năi ter gôr yòo têe-nêe láew

....

Exercise 2

Say these sentences in Thai.
พูดประโยคต่อไปนี้เป็นภาษาไทย

1. Speak slowly.
2. Drive a car quickly.
3. Children like to play game.
4. My house is very close to you.
5. You have a very small pet.

TSL4U

Fun Fact: 3 repeated words in Thai that mean 'easy' : 'กล้วย ๆ' 'หมู ๆ' and 'จิ๊บ ๆ'

1. กล้วย (glûuay) on its own means 'banana' and it can also be a symbol of 'easy' coming from an idiom "ง่ายเหมือนปลอกกล้วยเข้าปาก" (ngâai-mĕuuan-bpòk-glûuay-kâo-bpàak) which means as easy as pealing a banana into your mouth. Therefore, the term 'กล้วย ๆ' (glûuay-glûuay) means something very easy.

2. หมู (mŏo) on its own means 'pork' or 'pig'. It is another symbol for 'easy' coming from an idiom "หมูในอวย" (mŏo-nai-uuay) which means 'pork in the pot'; this is easy to eat because it's already in the pot and being cooked. So when you hear the term 'หมู ๆ' (mŏo-mŏo) ; it simply means 'very easy'.

3. จิ๊บ ๆ (jíp-jíp) refers to the sound of chicken in an idiom 'ลูกไก่ในกำมือ' (lôok-gài-nai-gam-meu) which means 'little chick in your hand'. As it cannot escape or run away, you can do anything with it. So the term 'จิ๊บ ๆ' (jíp-jíp) is referring to something under control or something easy to get done.

Challenge: You are at a coffee shop and want to order 1 iced green tea in a medium cup, less sweet, with extra ice; and want to pay with cash.

Chapter 4

เสาร์อาทิตย์นี้ทำอะไร

Săo-aa-tít-née tam-à-rai

What are you doing this weekend?

ที่ทำงาน Têe-tam-ngaan

1 แล้วคุณล่ะ เสาร์อาทิตย์นี้จะทำอะไร
Láew-kun-lâ
Săo-aa-tít-née-jà-tam-à-rai
2 ผมมีนัดกินข้าวกับเพื่อนครับ
Pŏm mee-nát-gin-kâao-
gàp-pêuuan kráp

1 เพื่อนที่เล่าให้ฟัง
คนที่เคยเรียนออสเตรเลียด้วยกันใช่มั้ย
Pêuuan-têe-lâo-hâi-fang
kon-têe-koiie-riian-
Australia-dûuay-gan châi-mái
2 คนนั้นแหละครับ นอกจากเพื่อนที่ทำงาน
ผมก็มีเธอแค่คนเดียวนี่แหละ
Kon-nán-làe kráp
Nôk-jàak pêuuan-têe-tam-ngaan
pŏm gôr mee-ter-kâe-kon-diieow-nêe-làe

English Translation

At work

Paul : What are you going to do this weekend?

Tee : I will take my family on a train ride to Kanchanaburi.

Paul : Is Kanchanaburi far?

Tee : Not that far. It only takes about 2-3 hours by train.

Paul : What is worth visiting in Kanchanaburi?

Tee : There are waterfalls, bamboo rafting, white water rafting, and then an old railway.

Tee : How about you? What are you going to do this weekend?

Paul : I have an appointment to eat out with friend.

Tee : The one you talked about- that she has studied in Australia with you, right?

Paul : That's the one. Apart from you guys at work, she is the only friend I have.

TSL4U

คำศัพท์ Vocabulary

Vocabulary	Definition	Note
พา paa	*Verb* [to] bring, lead, guide	
 **ครอบครัว** krôp-kruua	*Noun* family	
ไปเที่ยว bpai-tîieow	*Adverb* [to] travel, tour, go out	
น่าเที่ยว nâa-tîieow	*Stative Verb; Adjective* worth visiting	
น่า nâa	*Prefix* UNTRANSLATABLE! We can't translate this meaning into a direct English equivalent. It's a prefix added to a verb or adjective, meaning "worthy of.... -ing" or "....-able".	*For example:* - น่ากิน (nâa-gin): [to be] tasty-looking - น่าอร่อย (nâa-à-ròi): [to be] appetizing - น่าดู (nâa-doo): [to be] attractive - น่าไป (nâa-bpai): [to be] worth going - น่ารัก (nâa-rák): [to be] cute, pretty - น่าเกลียด (nâa-glìiat): [to be] disgusting, unattractive
กาญจนบุรี gaan-jà-ná-bù-ree	*Noun* Kanchanaburi	

TSL4U

คำศัพท์ Vocabulary

Vocabulary	Definition	Note
เอง eng	*Adverb* only, alone, just	As 'เอง' (eng) by itself means 'alone'; it can also be used at the end of sentence in equivalent to reflex pronoun in English. For example: - ฉันทำเค้กเอง (Chăn tam-kék eng) I make cake myself. - เขาไปซื้อของเอง (Kăo bpai-séu-kŏng eng) He go to buy think himself
บ้าง bâang	*Conjunction* some, any	
 น้ำตก náam-dtòk	*Noun* waterfall	
 ล่องแพ lông-pae	*Verb* [to] go bamboo rafting	
 ล่องแก่ง lông-gàeng	*Verb* [to] go white water rafting	
 ทางรถไฟ taang-rót-fai	*Noun* railroad, railway	

TSL4U

คำศัพท์ Vocabulary

Vocabulary	Definition	Note
นัด nát	*Noun; Classifier* 1. appointment *Verb* 2. [to] make an appointment	
มีนัด mee-nát	*Combined words* [to] have an appointment	
เล่า lâo	*Verb* [to] tell, describe, say	
ให้ hâi	*Verb* [to] give, offer [to] let, have	
เล่าให้ฟัง lâo-hâi-fang	*Combined words* [to] tell (someone) about (something)	
แหละ làe	*Particle* We can't translate this meaning into a direct English equivalent. It's a particle giving a sense of "this/that very one, exactly this/that one, this/that one in particular."	
นอกจาก nôk-jàak	*Preposition* apart from, except for, other than	

คำศัพท์ Vocabulary

Vocabulary	Definition	Note
เพื่อนที่ทำงาน pêuuan-têe-tam-ngaan	*Noun* colleague, co-worker, associate	
แค่ kâe	*Adverb Auxiliary* just, only	
เดียว diieow	*Quantifier* only, sole	
แค่คนเดียว kâe-kon-diieow	*Combined words* only one person, only person	

Exercise 1 What are these people doing this weekend?
เสาร์อาทิตย์นี้ พวกเขาทำอะไร

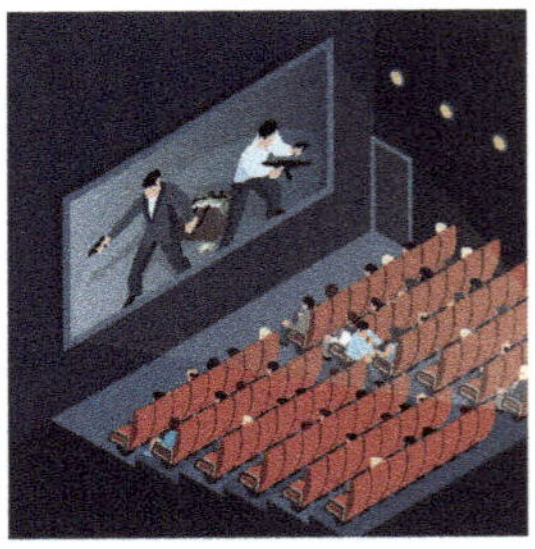

Exercise 2 Translate these sentences into Thai.
แปลประโยคต่อไปนี้เป็นภาษาไทย

1. Where are you going this weekend?

   ....

2. I will take my girlfriend to Phuket.

   ....

3. Phuket is not far from Krabi.

   ....

4. Pattaya is far from Bangkok about 2 hours.

   ....

5. Whom do you have appointment with?

   ....

Grammar 1

เสาร์อาทิตย์นี้

Săo-aa-tít-née

This weekend.

Structure: noun + นี้ (née)

Explanation: 'นี้' (née with high tone) means 'this' and it is an adjective placing after the noun to demonstrate the noun's specification. The common structure works for most nouns – and must be used with people in all cases. However, the classifiers can be omitted for some nouns – such as object and place. In the latter, the structure 'this noun' in English will be 'noun + 'นี้' (née)' only.

Time is an interesting one, the words 'วัน' (wan) day 'เดือน' (deuuan) month 'ปี' (bpee) year 'ชั่วโมง' (chûua-mohng) hour 'นาที' (naa-tee) minute or 'เวลา' (way-laa) time and 'ตอน' (dton) 'the period of time' can be both noun and a unit of time or classifier. So we always use 'time + 'นี้ (née)' to refer to 'this time' in English.

Please see below for examples:

Type of noun	Example
People	ครูคนนี้ (Kroo-kon-née) This teacher. น้องคนนี้ (Nóng-kon-née) This young person.
Place	บ้านหลังนี้ (bâan-lăng-née) This house. ถนนสายนี้ (Tà-nŏn-săai-née) This road.
Object	น้ำแก้วนี้ (Náam-gâew-née) This glass of water. รถคันนี้ (rót-kan-née) This car.
Time	วันนี้ (Wan-née) Today. เช้านี้ (Cháo-née) This morning. ตอนนี้ (Dton-née) At this moment; now

These are common classifiers in Thai.

Noun	Classifier
 Classifier for animals and anything with arm or legs	ตัว (dtuua)
 Classifier for person or people	คน (kon)
 Classifier for small objects such as toys and tools	อัน (an)
 Classifier for a piece of something – especially fabric and food	ชิ้น chín
 Classifier for fruit, ball, hill, mountain, storm, hurricane	ลูก (lôok)

Noun	Classifier
 Classfier for book, candle, knife	เล่ม (lêm)
 Classifier for plate, leaf, card, ticket, bag, hat, pot, pan, glass, cup	ใบ (bai)
 Classifier for vehicles (car, taxi, bike, motorbike, bus) ,umbrella, spoon	คัน (kan)
 Classifier for airplane, boat, cruise	ลำ (lam)
 Classifier for train, tram, parade	ขบวน (kà-buuan)

Noun	Classifier
 Classifier for house, piano	หลัง (lăng)
 Classifier for stone, lump, chunk, bar of soap	ก้อน (gôn)
 Classifier for mobile phone, computer, TV, game player, fridge, air-conditioner, heater, fan, washing machine, dryer	เครื่อง (krêuuang)
 Classifier for rice, food	จาน (jaan)
 Classifier for drink	แก้ว (gâew)
 Classifier for noodle, soup, sauce	ถ้วย (tûuay)

Exercise 1

Read Thai sentences and translate them into English.
อ่านประโยคภาษาไทยและแปลเป็นภาษาอังกฤษ

1.) บัตรเครดิตใบนี้
Bàt-kray-dìt bai née

....

2.) มอเตอร์ไซค์คันนี้
Mor-dtêr-sai kan née

....

3.) เดือนนี้
Deuuan née

....

4.) ชาไทยแก้วนี้หวานน้อย
Chaa-tai gâew née wăan-nói

....

5.) เค้กชิ้นนี้ไม่ค่อยอร่อย
Cake chín née mâi-kôi à-ròi

....

Exercise 2

Say these sentences in Thai.
พูดประโยคต่อไปนี้เป็นภาษาไทย

1. This year
2. This ticket
3. This mobile phone
4. This car is expensive.
5. I like this book.

Grammar 2

น่าเที่ยว

Nâa-tîieow

Worth visiting.

Structure: 'น่า' (nâa) + verb or adjective

Explanation: 'น่า' (nâa) is a prefix added to a verb or an adjective, meaning "worthy of doing" or "....-able" in Enlish.

For example:

Verb / Adjective	'น่า' (nâa) + Verb / Adjective
กิน (gin): [to] eat	น่ากิน (nâa-gin): [to be] tasty-looking
อร่อย (à-ròi): [to be] delicious	น่าอร่อย (nâa-à-ròi): [to be] appetizing
ดู (doo): [to] watch	น่าดู (nâa-doo): [to be] attractive
ไป (bpai): [to] go	น่าไป (nâa-bpai): [to be] worth going
รัก (rák): [to] love	น่ารัก (nâa-rák): [to be] cute; pretty
เกลียด (gliiat): [to] hate	น่าเกลียด (nâa-gliiat): [to be] disgusting; unattractive

Exercise 1

Read Thai sentences and translate them into English.
อ่านประโยคภาษาไทยและแปลเป็นภาษาอังกฤษ

1.) สัตว์เลี้ยงของคุณน่ารัก
Sàt-líiang kǒng-kun nâa-rák

....

2.) หนังเรื่องนี้น่าสนุก
Năng-rêuuang-née nâa-sà-nùk

....

3.) เขาพูดน่าฟัง
Kǎo pôot nâa-fang

....

4.) ส้มตำใส่พริกเยอะไม่น่ากิน
Sôm-dtam sài-prík-yúh mâi-nâa-gin

....

5.) ร้านนี้มีอะไรน่ากิน
Ráan-née mee à-rai nâa-gin

....

Exercise 2

Say these sentences in Thai.
พูดประโยคต่อไปนี้เป็นภาษาไทย

1. This house is livable.
2. Your daughter is lovely (cute, pretty).
3. Shabu Shabu at this shop is appetizing (tasty looking).
4. This book is worth-reading.
5. Is your country worth-visiting?

TSL4U

Grammar 3

มีอะไรน่าเที่ยวบ้าง
Mee à-rai nâa-tîieow bâang
What is worth visiting?

Structure: opened question + 'บ้าง' (bâang)

Explanation: 'บ้าง' (bâang) uses with questions that could have more than one answer, and you ask for a list of them.

Note: the informal pronunciation is มั่ง (mâng)

For example:

Formal	Informal
เอาอะไรบ้าง Ao à-rai bâang	เอาอะไรมั่ง Ao à-rai mâng
มีใครไปบ้าง Mee krai bpai bâang	มีใครไปมั่ง Mee krai bpai mâng
ซื้ออะไรมาบ้าง Séu à-rai maa bâang	ซื้ออะไรมามั่ง Séu à-rai maa mâng
คุณเป็นยังไงบ้าง Kun bpen yang-ngai bâang	คุณเป็นยังไงมั่ง Kun bpen yang-ngai mâng
คุณชอบอันไหนบ้าง Kun chôp an-năi bâang	คุณชอบอันไหนมั่ง Kun chôp an-năi mâng

Exercise 1 Read Thai sentences and translate them into English.
อ่านประโยคภาษาไทยและแปลเป็นภาษาอังกฤษ

1.) แม่พูดว่าอะไรบ้าง
Mâe pôot wâa à-rai bâang

....

2.) พ่อต้องกินยาเมื่อไหร่บ้าง
Pôr dtông gin yaa mêuua-rài bâang

....

3.) ใครทำงานวันเสาร์อาทิตย์บ้าง
Krai tam-ngaan wan-săo-aa-tít bâang

....

4.) เรียนภาษาไทยเป็นยังไงบ้าง
Riian paa-săa-tai bpen yang-ngai bâang

....

5.) คุณเคยไปเที่ยวที่ไหนในประเทศไทยบ้าง
Kun koiie bpai tîieow têe-năi nai bprà-têt-tai bâang

....

Exercise 2 Say these sentences in Thai – using the structure opened question + 'บ้าง' (bâang)
พูดประโยคต่อไปนี้เป็นภาษาไทย – โดยใช้โครงสร้าง ประโยคคำถามปลายเปิด + บ้าง

1. How are you today?
2. What language do you speak?
3. Who can drive?
4. Where does this bus go?
5. When do you have time?

Did you know?

ทางรถไฟเก่า' (taang-rót-fai-gào) the old railway is known as "The Death Railway", "The Burma Railway" and "The River Kwai Railway". It is the most famous train journey in Thailand, which runs from Bangkok to Kanchanaburi.

Here are some more details about the Death Railway:

- Construction began in 1942 under the order of the Imperial Japanese Army to connect Thailand (then Siam) and Burma (now Myanmar) in order to support the Japanese invasion of British India.
- The 415-kilometer railway line was built through extremely challenging jungle terrain, requiring the labor of over 60,000 POWs (Prisoner of war) and 200,000 civilians, many of whom died from disease, malnutrition, and exhaustion.
- Conditions for the workers were brutal, with inadequate food, shelter and medical care. It's estimated that over 12,000 POWs and 90,000 civilians died during the construction.
- After the war, much of the railway was abandoned, but sections have been rebuilt and restored as tourist attractions, including the famous "Death Railway" section.
- Today, the Death Railway and the River Kwai Bridge are important historical sites that draw visitors from around the world to learn about this tragic chapter of World War II history.

Challenge: Talk about your plan this weekend – including what are you going to do? Whom are you going with? How are you planning to go? And what is worth-going?

Chapter 5

ชาบูหรือหมูกระทะ

Chaa-boo rěu mŏo-grà-tá

Hot pot or BBQ?

1
Hot pot ที่เมืองไทยอร่อยมากครับ
โดยเฉพาะน้ำจิ้มกับน้ำซุป
Hot pot têe-meuuang-tai
à-ròi-mâak kráp
Doi-chà-pór náam-jîm gàp náam-súp
2
ที่จริงชาบูเป็นอาหารญี่ปุ่นนะ
ถ้า Hot Pot ของไทยแท้ ๆ เราเรียกว่าจิ้มจุ่ม
Têe-jing chaa-boo bpen
aa-hăan-yêe-bpùn ná
Tâa hot pot kŏng-tai-táe-táe
rao rîiak-wâa jîm-jùm

1
ถ้าเป็นจิ้มจุ่มแบบดั้งเดิม เราจะกินในหม้อดินเผา
น้ำซุปทำมาจากสมุนไพรไทย
ส่วนน้ำจิ้มก็จะเผ็ดและแซ่บกว่านี้
Tâa bpen jîm-jùm-bàep-dâng-derm
rao jà gin-nai-môr-din-păo
Náam-súp tam-maa-jàak sà-mŭn-prai-tai
Sùuan náam-jîm gôr jà pèt-láe-sâep gwàa-née
2
ว้าว วันหลังเราไปกินกันนะครับ
Wáao Wan-lăng
rao bpai-gin-gan ná-kráp

English Translation

Săen-dee : Do you want to eat Shabu or Moograta?

Paul : I don't know both. You can choose.

Săen-dee : Shabu is Hot Pot.
Moograta is BBQ.
Which one do you like?

Paul : Hot Pot in Thailand is very delicious.
Especially, dipping sauce and broth.

Săen-dee : Actually, shabu is Japanese food. If real Thai-style hot pot is called Jim-Jum.

Săen-dee : If it is the traditional Jim-jum, we will eat in a clay pot.
The broth is made from Thai herbs.
As for the dipping sauce, it is spicier and more delicious.

Paul : Wow, let's go and eat it together later.

คำศัพท์ Vocabulary

Vocabulary	Definition	Note
อยาก yàak	*Verb* [to] want to	
 **ชาบู** chaa-boo	*Noun* Shabu Shabu (a popular kind of Japanese hot pot dish)	
 **กระทะ** grà-tá	*Noun* pan, frying pan	
 **หมูกระทะ** mŏo-grà-tá	*Noun* Thai-style BBQ	
อย่าง yàang	*Noun; Classifier* 1. way, sort, variety *Adverb* 2. as, like	
ทั้ง 2 อย่าง tang-sŏng-yàang	*Combined word* both	

TSL4U

คำศัพท์ Vocabulary

Vocabulary	Definition	Note
เลือก lêuuak	*Verb* [to] choose, select, pick	
คือ keu	*Verb* [to be]	
Hot pot hot pot	*Noun* Hot pot	
BBQ BBQ	*Noun* BBQ	
แบบ bàep	*Noun; Classifier* model, style, way	
แบบไหน bàep-năi	*Combined words* What kind?	
โดยเฉพาะ doi-chà-pór	*Adverb* specially, especially, particularly	

คำศัพท์ Vocabulary

Vocabulary	Definition	Note
 **น้ำจิ้ม** náam-jîm	*Noun* dipping sauce	
 **น้ำซุป** náam-súp	*Noun* broth	
ที่จริง têe-jing	*Adverb* actually, in fact, in truth	
 **อาหาร** aa-hăan	*Noun* food	
 **ญี่ปุ่น** yêe-bpùn	*Noun* Japan	
อาหารญี่ปุ่น aa-hăan-yêe-bpùn	*Combined words* Japanese food	

คำศัพท์ Vocabulary

Vocabulary	Definition	Note
แท้ táe	*Adjective; Adverb* true, real, genuine	
เรียกว่า rîiak-wâa	*Verb* [to be] called, be named	
 **จิ้มจุ่ม** jîm-jùm	*Noun* Thai-style hot pot	
ดั้งเดิม dâng-derm	*StativeVerb ; Adjective* [to be] traditional, customary, original	
 **หม้อดินเผา** môr-din-pǎo	*Noun* clay pot	
ทำมาจาก tam-maa-jàak	*Combined words* made from	

คำศัพท์ Vocabulary

Vocabulary	Definition	Note
 **สมุนไพร** sà-mŭn-prai	*Noun* herb	
ส่วน sùuan	*Noun* part, portion, component *Conjunction* as for, for	
แซ่บ sâep	*Verb* [to be] delicious, be tasty	
แซ่บกว่านี้ sâep-gwàa-née	*Combined words* [to be] more delicious	
ว้าว wáao	*Interjection* wow!	
วันหลัง wan-lăng	*Noun* future, following day, later	

Exercise 1 Complete sentences with correct words.

เติมคำในช่องว่างด้วยคำที่ถูกต้อง

- หม้อดินเผา (mŏr-din-păo)
- อยาก (yaak)
- อร่อย (à-rŏi)
- น้ำซุป (náam-súp)
- น้ำจิ้ม (náam-jîm)
- นาน (naan)

1. ผม .... กินจิ้มจุ่มมา .... แล้ว
   Pŏm .... gin jîm-jùm maa .... láew

2. จิ้มจุ่ม .... มากโดยเฉพาะ .... กับน้ำซุป
   Jîm-jùm .... mâak doi-chà-pór .... gàp náam-súp

3. จิ้มจุ่มแบบดั้งเดิมต้องกินใน ....
   Jîm-jùm bàep dâng-derm dtông gin nai ....

4. .... ทำมาจากสมุนไพรไทย
   .... tam-ma-jàak sà-mŭn-prai-tai

Exercise 2 Make sentences using these words.
แต่งประโยคจากคำที่กำหนด

1.) อยากกิน (yàak-gin)

....

2.) เผ็ด (pèt)

....

3.) อร่อย (à-ròi)

....

4.) หรือ (rĕu)

....

5.) ไม่รู้จัก (mâi-róo-jàk)

....

TSL4U

Grammar 1

คุณอยากกินชาบูหรือหมูกระทะ

Kun yàak-gin chaa-boo rěu mŏo-grà-tá

Do you want to eat Shabu or Moograta?

Structure: อยาก (yàak) + Verb

Explanation: There are 2 common words for 'want' in Thai.

(1) 'อยาก' (yàak) is used when you want an action. For example: อยากไป (yàak-bpai) Want to go.

(2) เอา (ao) is used when you want an object – which we will learn in the next grammar. For example: เอาขนม (ao kà-nŏm) Want snacks.

Therefore, 'อยาก' (yàak) is always followed by another verb.

For example:

1. ฉันอยากกินชาบู
   Chăn yàak-gin chaa-boo
   I want to eat Shabu.

2. คุณอยากกินชาบูมั้ย
   Kun yàak-gin chaa-boo mái
   Do you want to eat Shabu?

3. ผมไม่อยากกินชาบู
   Pŏm mâi-yàak-gin chaa-boo
   I don't want to eat Shabu.

4. คุณอยากกินอะไร
   Kun yàak-gin à-rai
   What do you want to eat?

5. ใครอยากกินชาบู (บ้าง)
   Krai yàak-gin chaa-boo (bâang)
   Who wants to eat Shabu?

Exercise 1

Read Thai sentences and translate them into English.
อ่านประโยคภาษาไทยและแปลเป็นภาษาอังกฤษ

1.) ผมอยากเรียนภาษาไทย
Pŏm yàak-riian paa-săa-tai

....

2.) ฉันอยากไปเมืองไทย
Chăn yàak-bpai meuuang-tai

....

3.) เขาอยากดูหนัง
Kăo yàak-doo năng

....

4.) คุณอยากนั่งรถไฟไปกาญจนบุรีมั้ย
Kun yàak-nâng rót-fai bpai gaan-jà-ná-bù-ree mái

....

5.) เพื่อนของฉันไม่อยากเดินไกล ๆ
Pêuuan-kŏng-chăn mâi-yàak-dern glai-glai

....

Exercise 2

Say these sentences in Thai.
พูดประโยคต่อไปนี้เป็นภาษาไทย

1. I want to go to Australia.
2. Do you want to go to Australia?
3. She doesn't want to go to Australia?
4. Where do you want to go?
5. Who wants to go to Australia?

Grammar 2

คุณเอาชาบูหรือหมูกระทะ

Kun ao chaa-boo rĕu mŏo-grà-tá

Do you want Shabu or Moograta?

Structure: เอา (ao) + noun

Explanation: "เอา" (ao) is to want or to take something at the present time. It is the word used when ordering foods or buying things.

If we want or wish for something that cannot be obtained at the present time; We will use the word "อยากได้" (yàak-dâai) – which we will learn in the next grammar.

For example:

1. ฉันเอาชาเย็น 1 แก้ว
   Chăn ao chaa-yen nèung gâew
   I want a glass of iced tea.

2. คุณเอาชาเย็นมั้ย
   Kun ao chaa-yen mái
   Do you want iced tea?

3. ผมไม่เอาชาเย็น
   Pŏm mâi-ao chaa-yen
   I don't want iced tea.

4. คุณเอาอะไร
   Kun ao à-rai
   What do you want?

5. ใครเอาชาเย็น (บ้าง)
   Krai ao chaa-yen (bâang)
   Who wants iced tea?

Exercise 1

Read Thai sentences and translate them into English.
อ่านประโยคภาษาไทยและแปลเป็นภาษาอังกฤษ

1.) ฉันเอาอันนี้
Chăn ao an-née

....

2.) ฉันไม่เอาอันนั้น
Chăn mâi-ao an-nán

....

3.) คุณเอากาแฟร้อนมั้ย
Kun ao gaa-fae-rón mái

....

4.) ฉันเอาเสื้อสีฟ้า 2 ตัว
Chăn ao sêuua sěe-fáa sŏng dtuua

....

5.) คุณเอาเสื้อตัวไหน
Kun ao sêuua dtuua năi

....

Exercise 2

Say these sentences in Thai.
พูดประโยคต่อไปนี้เป็นภาษาไทย

1. I want iced coffee.
2. I don't want iced tea.
3. Do you want iced tea?
4. What do you want?
5. How many glasses of iced coffee do you want?

Grammar 3

ฉันอยากได้น้ำจิ้มแซ่บ ๆ

Chăn yàak-dâai náam-jîm sâep-sâep

I want to get tasty dipping sauce.

Structure: อยากได้ (yàak-dâai) + noun

Explanation: "อยากได้" (yàak-dâai) is a feeling of wanting to get, to have, or to obtain something. It doesn't necessarily mean you will get it, or plan to get it; you just want it. You can use the word "อยากได้" (yàak-dâai) for things that you feel wanting e.g. coffee, tea or a dipping sauce; or for things that you wish for e.g. a big house, a cool car or a diamond ring.

For example:

1. ฉันอยากได้น้ำจิ้มแซ่บ ๆ
   Chăn yàak-dâai náam-jîm sâep-sâep
   I want to get tasty dipping sauce.

2. คุณอยากได้น้ำจิ้มมั้ย
   Kun yàak-dâai náam-jîm mái
   Do you want to get tasty dipping sauce?

3. ผมไม่อยากได้น้ำจิ้ม
   Pŏm mâi-yàak-dâai náam-jîm
   I don't want tasty dipping sauce.

4. คุณอยากได้อะไร (บ้าง)
   Kun yàak-dâai à-rai (bâang)
   What do you want to get?

5. ใครอยากได้น้ำจิ้ม (บ้าง)
   Krai yàak-dâai náam-jîm (bâang)
   Who wants dipping sauce?

Exercise 1

Read Thai sentences and translate them into English.
อ่านประโยคภาษาไทยและแปลเป็นภาษาอังกฤษ

1.) ฉันอยากได้งานดี ๆ
Chăn yàak-dâai ngaan dee-dee

....

2.) ฉันไม่อยากได้เสื้อตัวนี้
Chăn mâi-yàak-dâai sêuua-dtuua-née

....

3.) คุณอยากได้หนังสือภาษาไทยมั้ย
Kun yàak-dâai năng-sĕu paa-săa-tai mái

....

4.) คุณไม่อยากได้โอทีเหรอ
Kun mâi-yàak-dâai OT rĕr

....

5.) ใครอยากได้โบนัสบ้าง
Krai yàak-dâai bonus bâang

....

Exercise 2

Say these sentences in Thai.
พูดประโยคต่อไปนี้เป็นภาษาไทย

1. I want to have a dog.
2. I don't want to have a cat.
3. Do you want to have a pet?
4. What pet do you want to have?
5. Which one do you want to have?

Fun fact:

Moograta's name is a playful combination of two words: 'หมู' (mŏo) which means 'pork' and 'กระทะ' (grà-tá) which means 'pan'.

While the name suggests pork as the primary ingredient, the menu is not limited to just pork. Chicken, beef, and even seafood can be part of the Moograta dining. The term Moograta has become more of a reference to the cooking method, its tasty dipping sauce and buffet style of dining.

Challenge: Say these sentences in Thai.

พูดประโยคต่อไปนี้เป็นภาษาไทย

1. I want to eat Moograta with you (and you only).
2. I don't want any chilli in my dipping sauce.
3. I want to have Moograta pan like this at home.

Chapter 6

สู้ ๆ

Sôo-sôo

(Keep) Fighting

พอลกับบอยที่ออฟฟิศ Paul gàp Boy têe office

1
งานคุณเสร็จหมดแล้วเหรอ
Ngaan kun sèt-mòt-láew-rěr
2
ยังไม่เสร็จหรอก แต่มันไม่ด่วนมาก
ผมมีประชุมกับทีมงานอีกทีตั้งอาทิตย์หน้า
Yang-mâi-sèt-ròk
dtàe man mâi-dùuan-mâak
Pǒm mee-bprà-chum-gàp-teem-ngaan
èek-tee dtâng aa-tít-nâa

1
คุณโชคดีจังเลย งานผมทั้งเยอะทั้งด่วน
Kun chôhk-dee-jang-loiie
Ngaan pǒm táng-yúh-táng-dùuan
2
สู้ ๆ นะครับ
Sôo-sôo ná-kráp
3
สู้ ๆ
Sôo-sôo

English Translation

At Office

Boy	:	Is it almost 5pm already!? My work hasn't finished yet.
Paul	:	Are there a lot left? Is there anything for me to help? Today, I am not quite busy.
Boy	:	A lot (totally a lot). Could you please help taking this report to the boss?
Paul	:	Sure, definitely.
Boy	:	Have you finished all your work?
Paul	:	No, I haven't. But it is not very urgent. I (will) have a meeting with the team again next week.
Boy	:	You are so lucky. My works are (all) a lot and (all) urgent.
Paul	:	Fighting!
Boy	:	Fighting!

คำศัพท์ Vocabulary

Vocabulary	Definition	Note
ให้ช่วย hâi-chûuay	*Combined words* [to be] helped	
เปล่า bplào	*NEG* 1. no, not *Stative Verb; Adjective* 2. [to be] empty, blank, vacant	
หรือเปล่า rěu-bplào	*Particle* or not	In spoken Thai, we say 'รึเปล่า' (réu-bplào).
ไม่ค่อย mâi-kôi	*Adverb* not really, not especially	
 ยุ่ง yûng	*Verb* 1. [to be] involved with, be mixed up with 2. [to] bother, disturb, interfere *Stative Verb; Adjective* 3. [to be] busy, hectic	
 รีพอร์ท report	*Verb* 1. [to] report *Noun* 2. a report	

TSL4U

คำศัพท์ Vocabulary

Vocabulary	Definition	Note
เอาไปให้ / เอา ...... ไปให้ ao-bpai-hâi	*Combined words* [to] go and give	
หัวหน้า hŭua-nâa	*Noun* boss, leader, chief	
หน่อย nòi	*Adverb* a little, a little bit	
ได้มั้ย dâai-mái	*Combined words* asking for ability – can or not?	
ได้เลย dâai-loiie	*Adverb* Sure, definitely	
หมด mòt	*Adverb* 1. completely, entirely *Stative Verb; Adjective* 2. [to be] finished, used up	
หรอก ròk	*Particle* UNTRANSLATABLE We can't translate this meaning into a direct English equivalent. It's a particle used in the negative when making a contradiction.	

คำศัพท์ Vocabulary

Vocabulary	Definition	Note
มัน man	*Personal Pronoun* 1. It 2. he, she, him, her (using มัน to mean he/she is regarded as being insulting, unless used by close friends.) *Stative Verb; Adjective* 3. [to be] glossy, shiny 4. [to be] fun, enjoyable 5. [to be] oily, greasy *Noun* 6. oil, grease, fat	
 ด่วน dùuan	*Stative Verb; Adjective* [to be] urgent, express	
 ประชุม bprà-chum	*Verb* 1. [to] meet, gather 2. [to] have a meeting, hold a meeting	Grammartically 'ประชุม' (bprà-chum) is a verb means 'to have a meeting' and the noun for 'a meeting' is 'การประชุม' (gaan bprà-chum) However, informally, it is common to hear people leave out the word 'การ' (gaan) and use 'ประชุม' (bpra-chum) only. This is why you see Paul said "ผมมีประชุมอาทิตย์หน้า" (pǒm mee bprà-chum aa-tít nâa) instead of "ผมมีการประชุมอาทิตย์หน้า" (pǒm mee gaan bprà-chum aa-tít nâa).
ทีมงาน teem-ngaan	*Noun* working team	
อีกที èek-tee	*Adverb* once more, one more time	

TSL4U

คำศัพท์ Vocabulary

Vocabulary	Definition	Note
ตั้ง dtâng	*Adverb* up to, as much as *Verb* [to] set, set up, establish	
หน้า nâa	*Preposition* 1. in front of, front *Noun* 2. face, front, top 3. season *Adjective* 4. next, following, upcoming *Noun; Classifier* 5. page	
อาทิตย์หน้า aa-tít-nâa	*Combined words* next week	
โชคดี chôhk-dee	*Interjection* Good luck!, Take care! *Stative Verb; Adjective* [to be] lucky, fortunate	
จังเลย jang-loiie	*Adverb* so much, extremely, greatly	
สู้ sôo	*Verb* [to] fight, oppose	
 สู้ๆ sôo-sôo	*Combined Words* Fighting!	

Exercise 1

Choose the correct answer.
เลือกคำตอบที่ถูกต้อง

1. ใกล้จะ 5 โมงแล้ว ใครยังทำงานไม่เสร็จ
   Glâi-jà-hâa-mohng-láew krai-yang-tam-ngaan-mâi-sèt

   a พอล Paul

   b บอย Boy

   c ทั้งสองคน Táng-sŏng-kon

2. บอยขอให้พอลช่วยทำอะไร
   Boy kŏr hâi Paul chûuay tam-à-rai

   a ซื้อชาเย็น Séu chaa-yen

   b พาไปกินหมูกระทะ Paa-bpai-gin mŏo-grà-tá

   c เอารีพอร์ทไปให้หัวหน้า Ao-report-bpai-hâi-hŭua-nâa

3. ทำไมพอลกลับบ้านตรงเวลาได้
   Tam-mai Paul glàp-bâan dtrong-way-laa dâai

   a พอลทำงานเสร็จหมดแล้ว Paul tam-ngaan sèt-mòt-láew

   b บอยช่วยพอลทำงาน Boy chûuay Paul tam-ngaan

   c งานของพอลไม่ด่วน Ngaan kŏng Paul mâi-dùuan

4. ข้อไหนถูก Kôr-năi-tòok
   Which sentence is correct?

   a 5 โมงแล้ว พอลยังทำงาน Hâa-mohng-láew Paul yang tam-ngaan

   b 5 โมงแล้ว บอยยังทำงาน Hâa-mohng-láew Boy yang tam-ngaan

   c 5 โมงแล้ว ไม่มีใครทำงานแล้ว Hâa-mohng-láew Mâi-mee-krai-tam-ngaan-láew

5. ข้อไหนถูก Kôr-năi-tòok
   Which sentence is correct?

   a งานของบอยด่วนแต่ไม่เยอะ Ngaan kŏng Boy dùuan dtàe mâi-yúh

   b งานของบอยเยอะแต่ไม่ด่วน Ngaan kŏng Boy yúh dtàe mâi-dùuan

   c งานของบอยทั้งเยอะทั้งด่วน Ngaan kŏng Boy táng-yúh táng-dùuan

Exercise 2

Put these words in the correct order.
เรียงคำให้เป็นประโยคที่ถูกต้อง

1. ยุ่ง ผม วันนี้ มาก
   yûng pǒm wan-née mâak

→ ……………………………………………………………………

2. ผม แต่งตัว เสร็จ ยัง แฟน ไม่
   pǒm dtàeng-dtuua sèt yang faen mâi

→ ……………………………………………………………………

3. หมด คุณ เสร็จ แล้ว ทำงาน เหรอ
   mòt kun sèt láew tam-ngaan rěr

→ ……………………………………………………………………

4. ไป ให้ หัวหน้า ได้ มั้ย เอา พิซซ่า ช่วย
   bpai hâi hǔua-nâa dâai mái ao pizza chûuay

→ ……………………………………………………………………

5. ทีมงาน อาทิตย์ หน้า ผม จะ เจอ อีกที
   teem-ngaan aa-tít nâa pǒm jà jer èek-tee

→ ……………………………………………………………………

Grammar 1

ได้เลย

Dâai-loiie

Sure, definitely.

Structure: sentence + เลย (loiie)

Explanation: เลย (loiie) is a particle word; usually found at the end of the sentence or phrase. It adds emphasis and intensity. It conveys a sense of 'so much, completely, totally' in a positive sense; or 'not at all, not even a bit' in the negative sense.

For example:

1. กินเลย
   Gin loiie
   Eat now.

2. กินเลยมั้ย
   Gin loiie mái
   Shall (we) eat now?

3. ไม่รู้เลย
   Mâi-róo loiie
   (I) don't know at all.

4. สวยจังเลย
   Sŭuay-jang loiie
   Very beautiful.

5. คนเยอะเลย
   Kon-yúh loiie
   A lot of people.

Exercise 1

Read Thai sentences and translate them into English.
อ่านประโยคภาษาไทยและแปลเป็นภาษาอังกฤษ

1.) เอาเลย
Ao loiie

....

2.) เอาเลยมั้ย
Ao loiie mái

....

3.) ร้อนจังเลย
Rón-jang loiie

....

4.) ไม่ร้อนเลย
Mâi-rón loiie

....

5.) ที่ตลาดมีขนมเยอะเลย
Têe dtà-làat mee kà-nŏm-yúh loiie

....

Exercise 2

Say these sentences in Thai.
พูดประโยคต่อไปนี้เป็นภาษาไทย

1. Let's go!!
2. Shall (we) go?
3. Very delicious.
4. Not delicious at all.
5. He doesn't have any Thai friend at all.

TSL4U

Grammar 2

มีอะไรให้ผมช่วยรึเปล่า
Mee-à-rai hâi pŏm chûuay réu bplào

Is there anything for me to help?

Structure: มี (mee) + อะไร (à-rai)

Explanation: มี (mee) has 2 meanings: (1) to have (2) there is, there are. อะไร (à-rai) has 2 meanings: (1) what – as a question word (2) something or anything – as a pronoun.

When combining the 2 words together, we get a new phrase: มีอะไร (mee-à-rai) which means "is there anything"; and if we add the negative word ไม่ (mâi) in front, we get the phase ไม่มีอะไร (mâi-mee-à-rai) means "there is nothing".

For example:

1. มีอะไร
   Mee-à-rai
   Is there anything?

2. ไม่มีอะไร
   Mâi-mee-à-rai
   There is nothing.

3. มีอะไรทำบ้าง
   Mee-à-rai tam bâang
   Is there anything (for me) to do?

4. ไม่มีอะไรทำ (เลย)
   Mâi-mee-à-rai tam (loiie)
   There is nothing (for me) to do.

5. ทำไมไม่มีอะไรทำ
   Tam-mai mâi-mee-à-rai tam
   Why don't you have anything to do?

Exercise 1

Read Thai sentences and translate them into English.
อ่านประโยคภาษาไทยและแปลเป็นภาษาอังกฤษ

1.) มีอะไรกินบ้าง
Mee-à-rai gin bâang

....

2.) ที่บ้านไม่มีอะไรกิน (เลย)
Têe bâan mâi-mee-à-rai gin (loiie)

....

3.) ที่ร้านอาหารมีอะไรน่ากิน
Têe ráan-aa-hăan mee-à-rai nâa-gin

....

4.) มีอะไรอีก
Mee-à-rai èek

....

5.) ไม่มีอะไรแล้ว
Mâi-mee-à-rai láew

....

Exercise 2

Say these sentences in Thai.
พูดประโยคต่อไปนี้เป็นภาษาไทย

1. I have nothing to say.
2. Do you have anything to tell?
3. I have nothing to do this weekend.
4. Is there anything for me to help?
5. Is there anything worth-travelling in Kanchanaburi?

TSL4U

Grammar 3

มีอะไรให้ผมช่วยรึเปล่า

Mee-à-rai hâi pŏm chûuay réu bplào

Is there anything for me to help?

Structure and Explanation:

ให้ (hâi) by itself means 'to give'; however it can be placed in a certain structure to give different meanings. The most common structures are:

(1) subject + ให้ (hâi) + object + person e.g. ฉันให้เงินแม่ (Chăn hâi ngern mâe) I give money to mum. In this structure, 'ให้' (hâi) means 'to give'.

(2) subject + verb + object + ให้ (hâi) + person e.g. ฉันจ่ายเงินให้แม่ (Chăn jàai ngern hâi mâe) I pay money for mum. 'ให้' (hâi) in this structure is used to convey the action of doing something 'for' someone.

(3) subject + ให้ (hâi) + person + verb e.g. แม่ให้ฉันจ่ายเงิน (Mâe hâi chăn jàai ngern) Mum lets me pay money. 'ให้' (hâi) in this structure means 'to let or to ask' someone to do something.

Note: We can make this sentence more polite by adding the word ขอ (kŏr) in front of ให้ (hâi) e.g. แม่ขอให้ฉันจ่ายเงิน (Mâe kŏr hâi chăn jàai ngern) Mum asks me to pay money.

(4) ขอ (kŏr) + ให้ (hâi) + sentence e.g. ขอให้โชคดี (Kŏr-hâi chôhk-dee) Wish you good luck. This combination of ขอ (kŏr) + ให้ (hâi) means 'to wish'.

For example:

1. หัวหน้าให้งานผม
   Hŭua-nâa hâi ngaan pŏm
   Boss gives work to me.

2. ผมทำงานให้หัวหน้า
   Pŏm tam-ngaan hâi hŭua-nâa
   I work for boss.

3. หัวหน้าให้ผมทำงาน
   Hŭua-nâa hâi pŏm tam-ngaan
   Boss asks me to work.

4. หัวหน้าขอให้ผมโชคดี
   Hŭua-nâa kŏr-hâi pŏm chôhk-dee
   Boss wishes me good luck.

5. ผมขอให้หัวหน้ามีความสุข
   Pŏm kŏr-hâi hŭua-nâa mee-kwaam-sùk
   I wish boss happiness.

Exercise 1

Read Thai sentences and translate them into English.
อ่านประโยคภาษาไทยและแปลเป็นภาษาอังกฤษ

1.) แม่ให้ขนมน้อง
Mâe hâi kà-nŏm nóng

....

2.) แม่ซื้อขนมให้น้อง
Mâe séu kà-nŏm hâi nóng

....

3.) แม่ให้น้องซื้อขนม
Mâe hâi nóng séu kà-nŏm

....

4.) แม่ไม่ให้น้องซื้อขนม
Mâe mâi-hâi nóng séu kà-nŏm

....

5.) ใครซื้อขนมให้น้อง
Krai séu kà-nŏm hâi nóng

....

Exercise 2

Say these sentences in Thai.
พูดประโยคต่อไปนี้เป็นภาษาไทย

1. Mum lets children play game.
2. Dad doesn't let children play game.
3. Who lets children play game?
4. Does dad let children play game?
5. What doesn't dad let children do?

Note: เด็ก (dèk) is a child, เด็ก ๆ (dèk-dèk) is children.

Fun Fact:

Thai workplace can be relationship-oriented, especially when comparing to the Westerners. Building and maintaining social relationships are important in Thai workplaces. Networking and socializing with colleagues outside of work hours are common practices and may influence professional relationships and opportunities.

Challenge: Make a sentence using these 3 words:
มีอะไร (mee-à-rai) ให้ (hâi) เลย (loiie)

Chapter 7

ตลาดนัดจตุจักร

Dtà-làat-nát-jà-dtù-jàk

Chatuchak market

ที่ตลาดนัดจตุจักร Têe dtà-làat-nát-jà-dtù-jàk

1
คุณสนใจอะไรเป็นพิเศษมั้ย
Kun sŏn-jai-à-rai-bpen-pí-sèt-mái
2
ผมอยากไปดูสัตว์เลี้ยงครับ ผมชอบหมามาก
Pŏm yàak bpai-doo sàt-líiang kráp
Pŏm chop măa mâak

1
ฉันก็ชอบหมามาก ที่บ้านมีโกลเด้น 1 ตัว
Chăn gôr chop măa mâak
Têe-bâan mee gol-dên nèung dtuua
2
เหมือนกันเลยครับ
บ้านผมที่ออสเตรเลียก็มีโกลเด้น 1 ตัว
Mĕuuan-gan-loiie kráp
Bâan pŏm têe Australia gôr mee
gol-dên nèung dtuua

English Translation

At Chatuchak market

Săen-dee : Have you ever been to Chatuchak market?

Paul : No, I haven't. What is interesting here?

Săen-dee : It has everything from food, clothes, pets

Săen-dee : plants, souvenirs, wedding souvenirs, amulets, plates and bowls, spoons and folks, home decoration.

Săen-dee : There are also opened-hat musicians.

Săen-dee : Are you particularly interested in anything?

Paul : I would like to see pets. I really like dogs.

Săen-dee : I also like dogs very much. I have 1 Golden Retriever at my house.

Paul : Me too. At my house in Australia, I also have 1 Golden Retriever.

คำศัพท์ Vocabulary

Vocabulary	Definition	Note
ตลาดนัด dtà-làat-nát	*Noun* market fair	'ตลาด' (dtà-làat) means 'market' and 'นัด' (nát) means 'appointment' so when combining the two words together, it means a market that set up according to the appointment. This type of markets is usually not permanent; but open on specific time (often on the weekends).
 **ตลาดนัดจตุจักร** dtà-làat-nát-jà-dtù-jàk	*Noun* Chatuchak market	
สนใจ sǒn-jai	*Verb* [to be] interested (in)	
น่าสนใจ nâa-sǒn-jai	*Stative Verb; Adjective* [to be] interesting	
ทุกอย่าง túk-yàang	*Indefinite Pronoun* everything, every kind, every thing	
ตั้งแต่ dtâng-dtàe	*Preposition* since, from	

คำศัพท์ Vocabulary

Vocabulary	Definition	Note
 **ไม้** mái	*Noun* 1. wood 2. stick	
 **ต้นไม้** dtôn-mái	*Noun* tree, plant	
ฝาก fàak	*Verb* [to] deposit, leave with somebody	
ของฝาก kǒng-fàak	*Noun* souvenir	
 **ของชำร่วย** kǒng-cham-rûuay	*Noun* wedding souvenir	

TSL4U

คำศัพท์ Vocabulary

Vocabulary	Definition	Note
 **พระ** prá	*Noun* 1. Buddha statue 2. monk	
เครื่อง krêuuang	*Noun; Classifier* machine, tool, engine	
 **พระเครื่อง** prá-krêuuang	*Noun* small Buddha, amulet	
 **ชาม** chaam	*Noun* bowl	
 **จานชาม** jaan-chaam	*Combined words* plates and bowls	
 **ช้อน** chón	*Noun* spoon	

คำศัพท์ Vocabulary

Vocabulary	Definition	Note
 **ส้อม** sôm	*Noun* fork	
ตกแต่ง dtòk-dtàeng	*Verb* [to] decorate, beautify	
ของตกแต่งบ้าน kŏng-dtòk-dtàeng-bâan	*Combined words* home decoration	
 **ดนตรี** don-dtree	*Noun* music	
นัก nák	*Prefix* UNTRANSLATABLE We can't translate this meaning into a direct English equivalent. It's used as prefix before nouns or verbs to describe a profession connected to that word.	For example: - นักเรียน (nák-riian): student - นักเขียน (nák-kĭian): author - นักร้อง (nák-róng): singer - นักกีฬา (nák-gee-laa): athlete - นักบาส (nák-bàat): basketball player - นักบอล (nák-bon): football player
 **นักดนตรี** nák-don-dtree	*Noun* musician	

คำศัพท์ Vocabulary

Vocabulary	Definition	Note
นักดนตรีเปิดหมวก nák-don-dtree-bpèrt-mùuak	*Combined words* opened-hat musician, busker	
พิเศษ pí-sèt	*Adverb* 1. specially, extraordinarily *Stative Verb; Adjective* 2. [to be] special, extraordinary	
ไปดู bpai-doo	*Combined words* [to] go and see	
 **หมา** mǎa	*Noun* dog	
เหมือนกันเลย měuuan-gan-loiie	*Combined words* It's the same; me too!	

Exercise 1 True or false.
ถูกหรือผิด

1.)………………… แสนดีกับพอลอยู่ที่ตลาดน้ำ
Săen-dee gàp Paul yòo têe dtà-làat-náam

2.)………………… พอลไม่เคยไปตลาดนัดจตุจักร
Paul mâi-koiie bpai dtà-làat-nát-jà-dtù-jàk

3.)………………… ที่ตลาดนัดจตุจักรไม่มีร้านขายสัตว์เลี้ยง
Têe dtà-làat-nát-jà-dtù-jàk mâi-mee
ráan-kăai-sàt- líiang

4.)………………… พอลอยากไปดูต้นไม้
Paul yàak bpai doo dtôn-mái

5.)………………… พอลกับแสนดีชอบหมาเหมือนกัน
Paul gàp Săen-dee chôp măa mĕuuan-gan

Exercise 2 Make sentences using these words.
แต่งประโยคจากคำที่กำหนด

1.) เคย (koiie)

....

2.) สนใจ (sŏn-jai)

....

3.) เหมือนกัน (mĕuuan-gan)

....

4.) ของฝาก (kŏng-fàak)

....

5.) พิเศษ (pí-sèt)

....

Grammar 1

คุณเคยมาตลาดนัดจตุจักรมั้ย
Kun koiie maa dtà-làat-nát jà-dtù-jàk mái

Have you ever been to Chatuchak market?

Structure: (subject) + เคย (koiie) + verb

Explanation: 'เคย' (koiie) is an adverb, means 'ever'. When referring to something has happened in the past, in Thai we use the word 'เคย' (koiie) for positive and 'ไม่เคย' (mâi-koiie) for negative statements.

For example:

1. คุณเคยมาตลาดนัดจตุจักรมั้ย
   Kun koiie maa dtà-làat-nát jà-dtù-jàk mái
   Have you ever been to Chatuchak market?
2. ผมเคยมาตลาดนัดจตุจักร
   Pŏm koiie maa dtà-làat-nát jà-dtù-jàk
   I have been to Chatuchak market.
3. ผมไม่เคยมาตลาดนัดจตุจักร
   Pŏm mâi-koiie maa dtà-làat-nát jà-dtù-jàk
   I have never been to Chatuchak market.
4. คุณไม่เคยมาตลาดนัดจตุจักรเหรอ
   Kun mâi-koiie maa dtà-làat-nát jà-dtù-jàk rĕr
   You have never been to Chatuchak market, have you?
5. คุณเคยไปที่ไหน (บ้าง)
   Kun koiie bpai têe-năi (bâang)
   Where have you been?

TSL4U

Exercise 1 Read Thai sentences and translate them into English.
อ่านประโยคภาษาไทยและแปลเป็นภาษาอังกฤษ

1.) คุณเคยกินหมูกระทะมั้ย
Kun koiie gin mŏo-grà-tá mái

....

2.) ฉันเคยกินหมูกระทะ
Chăn koiie gin mŏo-grà-tá

....

3.) ฉันไม่เคยกินหมูกระทะ
Chăn mâi-koiie gin mŏo-grà-tá

....

4.) คุณไม่เคยกินหมูกระทะเหรอ
Kun mâi-koiie gin mŏo-grà-tá rĕr

....

5.) ใครเคยกินหมูกระทะ
Krai koiie gin mŏo-grà-tá

....

Exercise 2 Say these sentences in Thai.
พูดประโยคต่อไปนี้เป็นภาษาไทย

1. Have you ever been to Kanchanaburi?
2. I have been to Kanchanaburi.
3. I have never been to Kanchanaburi.
4. You have never been to Kanchanaburi, have you?
5. Where in Thailand have you been?

Grammar 2

ฉันก็ชอบหมา

Chăn gôr chôp măa

I also like dogs.

Explanation Structure and Examples:

1. The most common use of 'ก็' (gôr) is as an adverb meaning 'also'.

Structure: Sentence 1: subject + verb + object
Sentence 2: subject + ก็ (gôr) + verb +object

Examples from the story are:

(1) นักดนตรีเปิดหมวกก็มีนะ
Nák-don-dtree-bpèrt-mùuak gôr mee ná
Opened-hat musicians also have.

(2) ฉันก็ชอบหมา
Chăn gôr chôp măa
I also like dogs.

(3) ผมก็มีโกลเด้น 1 ตัว
Pŏm gôr mee golden nèung dtuua
I also have 1 Golden Retriever.

However, 'ก็' (gôr) also have other uses as following:

2. As a conjunction means 'then, so, therefore'

Structure: cause + ก็ (gôr) + effect

For examples:

(1) หิวก็กิน
Hĭw-gôr-gin
Hungry, then eat.

(2) ไม่หิวก็ไม่ต้องกิน
Mâi-hĭw gôr mâi-dtông-gin
If not hungry, then don't have to eat.

(3) ชอบเขาก็บอกเขา
Chôp-kăo gôr bòk-kăo
Like him, then tell him.

3. Very rarely and casually, 'ก็' (gôr) can also be used as a conjunction meaning 'because'.

Structure: effect+ ก็ (gôr) + cause

For examples:

(1) ฉันไม่รู้ ก็เขาไม่เคยบอก
Chǎn-mâi-róo · gôr kǎo-mâi-koiie-bòk
I don't know because he never told (me).

(2) เขาไม่เคยบอก ก็คิดว่าเธอรู้แล้ว
Kǎo-mâi-koiie-bòk · gôr kít-wâa ter-róo-láew
He has never told (her), because (he) thinks that she already knew.

(3) Q: ทำไมเมื่อวานไม่มา A: ก็ฉันไม่สบาย
Q: Tam-mai mêuua-waan mâi maa A: Gôr chǎn mâi-sà-baai
Q: Why didn't (you) come yesterday? A: Because I wasn't well.

Note: This is a very rare use of "gor". We include in this grammar so you can understand- if you every come across. However, as an intermediate Thai speakers, we commend you use the word เพราะ (prór) as it is easier and more recommend.

Exercise 1

Read Thai sentences and translate them into English.
อ่านประโยคภาษาไทยและแปลเป็นภาษาอังกฤษ

1.) (เขาไม่เคยไปตลาดนัดจตุจักร) ผมก็ไม่เคยไปตลาดนัดจตุจักร
(Kăo mâi-koiie bpai dtà-làat-nát-jà-dtù-jàk) Pŏm gôr mâi-koiie bpai dtà-làat-nát-jà-dtù-jàk

....

2.) (ผมชอบหมา) คุณก็ชอบหมาเหรอ
(Pŏm chôp măa) Kun gôr chôp măa rĕr

....

3.) เหนื่อยก็พัก
Nèuuay-gôr-pák

....

4.) ซื้อก็ดี ไม่ซื้อก็ได้
Séu gôr-dee mâi-séu gôr-dâai

....

5.) (ทำไมไม่ซื้อ) ก็เงินเดือนยังไม่ออก
(Tam-mai mâi-séu) Gôr ngern-deuuan yang-mâi-òk

....

Exercise 2

Say these sentences in Thai.
พูดประโยคต่อไปนี้เป็นภาษาไทย

1. (She likes trees.) I also like trees.
2. (He is a musician.) I am also a musician.
3. Yesterday I ate noodle, today I also eat noodle.
4. If you are hot, then turn on the air conditioner.
5. (Why do you like Chatujak market?) Because it has everything.

Grammar 3

โกลเด้น 1 ตัว

Gol-dên nèung dtuua

1 Golden Retriever

Structure and Explanation:

Thai classifiers are units of nouns – similar to units of uncountable nouns in English. For example: 'a glass of water' in Thai we say 'น้ำ 1 แก้ว' (náam-nèung-gâew). However, in Thai language, we have classifier words for both - countable and uncountable - nouns. When referring to quantity or amount of any noun, we always follow structure:

noun + number + classifier

If you do not know the quantity or amount, and would like to ask a question; then follow this structure:

noun + กี่ (gèe) + classifier

Please refer to table in chapter 4 for common classifiers in Thai.

For example:

1. ต้นไม้ 1 ต้น
   Dtón-mái nèung dtôn
   1 tree

2. ครู 2 คน
   Kroo sǒng kon
   2 teachers

3. ผลไม้ 3 ลูก
   Pǒn-lá-mái sǎam look
   3 fruits

4. บ้าน 4 หลัง
   Bâan sèe lǎng
   4 houses

5. วันหยุดกี่วัน
   Wan-yùt gèe wan
   How many days is the holiday?

TSL4U

Exercise 1

Read Thai sentences and translate them into English.
อ่านประโยคภาษาไทยและแปลเป็นภาษาอังกฤษ

1.) เงิน 5 บาท
Ngern hâa bàat

....

2.) รถยนต์ 6 คัน
Rót-yon hòk kan

....

3.) กระเป๋า 7 ใบ
Grà-bpǎo jèt bai

....

4.) บ้านผมมีปลา 8 ตัว
Bâan-pǒm mee bplaa bpàet dtuua

....

5.) คุณมีเพื่อนกี่คน
Kun mee pêuuan gèe-kon

....

Exercise 2

Say these sentences in Thai.
พูดประโยคต่อไปนี้เป็นภาษาไทย

1. 9 mobile phones.
2. 10 glasses of orange juice.
3. 11 bowls of soup.
4. How many bowls of dipping sauce?
5. How many hours do you work today?

Fun Fact:

An idiom for 'having everything' in Thai is "ตั้งแต่สากเบือยันเรือรบ" (dtâng-dtàe sàak-ka-beuua yan-reuua-róp) which literally means "from pestle to battleship". In other words, it implies that from very small thing (pestle) to very big thing (battleship).

In some regions, you may hear "ตั้งแต่ไม้จิ้มฟันยันเรือรบ" (dtâng-dtàe mái-jîm-fan yan-reuua-róp) which means "from toothpick to battleship".

From the story, instead of saying "ตลาดนัดจตุจักรมีทุกอย่าง ตั้งแต่อาหาร เสื้อผ้า สัตว์เลี้ยง ต้นไม้ ของฝาก ของชำร่วย พระเครื่อง จานชาม ช้อนส้อม ของตกแต่งบ้าน นักดนตรีเปิดหมวกก็มีนะ" (Dtà-làat-nát-jà-dtù-jàk mee-túk-yàang dtâng-dtàe aa-hăan sêuua-pâa sàt-líiang dtôn-mái kŏng-fàak kŏng-cham-rûuay prá-krêuuang jaan-chaam chón-sôm kŏng-dtòk-dtàeng-bâan nák-don-dtree-bpèrt-mùuak gôr mee ná)

Thai people could say "ตลาดนัดจตุจักรมีทุกอย่างตั้งแต่สากเบือยันเรือรบ" (Dtà-làat-nát-jà-dtù-jàk mee-túk-yàang dtâng-dtàe sàak-ka-beuua-yan-reuua-róp) to make the sentence shorter and convey the same meaning.

Challenge: Make your own sentence using the idiom "ตั้งแต่สากเบือยันเรือรบ" (dtâng-dtàe sàak-ka-beuua yan-reuua-róp)

Chapter 8

กินอะไรดี

Gin-à-rai-dee

What shall we eat?

ที่ออฟฟิศ Têe office

1 แล้วร้านอาหารตามสั่งหน้าปากซอยล่ะ
Láew ráan-aa-hăan-dtaam-sàng nâa-bpàak-soi lâ
2 ดีครับ มีให้เลือกหลายอย่างเลย
Dee-kráp Mee-hâi-lêuuak-lăai-yàang-loiie
3 ไม่ต้องเดินไกลด้วย
Mâi-dtông-dern-glai dûuay
4 แอร์เย็นด้วย
Ae-yen dûuay

1 ฉันจะได้แวะซื้อน้ำปั่นที่ร้านข้าง ๆ ด้วย
Chăn jà dâai wáe-séu náam-bpàn têe ráan kâang-kâang dûuay
2 เมื่อกี้ใครบอกว่าลดความอ้วนอยู่
mêuua-gêe krai bòk wâa lót-kwaam-ûuan-yòo

English Translation

At the office.

John	:	This noon, shall we go and eat Hainanese chicken rice together?
Jane	:	No, I am in process of losing weight (I am on diet now).
Jay	:	Then, let's go to the cafeteria. There are many things to choose.
Paul	:	No. I think it's too hot.
John	:	Then shall we go to the food court in a department store? So there is a cool air.
Jane	:	No. It is far. I am too lazy to walk.
Jay	:	How about the made-to-order restaurant at the entrance of the side street?
John	:	That's good. There are many things to choose.
Jane	:	(We) don't have to take a long walk as well.
Paul	:	The air is also cool.
Jane	:	And I can stop by to buy a smoothie at the shop next door.
Paul / John / Jay	:	A moment ago, who said that (I am) in process of losing weight?

คำศัพท์ Vocabulary

Vocabulary	Definition	Note
 เที่ยง tîiang	*Noun* noon, midday	
 ข้าวมันไก่ kâao-man-gài	*Noun* Hainanese chicken rice	
 ลดความอ้วน lót-kwaam-ûuan	*Verb* [to] diet, lose weight	
ลด lót	*Verb* [to] lower, reduce, decrease	
 อ้วน ûuan	*Stative Verb ; Adjective* [to be] fat, overweight	
ความ kwaam	*Prefix* UNTRANSLATABLE We can't translate this meaning into a direct English equivalent. It's a prefix which converts a verb or adjective (relating to thoughts and feelings) into an abstract noun.	*For example:* - ความรู้ (kwaam-róo): knowledge - ความคิด (kwaam-kít): thought, idea - ความจริง (kwaam-jing): truth, fact - ความเห็น (kwaam-hěn): view point, opinion - ความรัก (kwaam-rák): love

คำศัพท์ Vocabulary

Vocabulary	Definition	Note
งั้น ngán	*Conjunction* if so, in that case, then	Another common combined word with 'งั้น' (ngán) is 'ไม่งั้น' (mâi ngán), which means otherwise.
โรงอาหาร rohng-aa-hăan	*Noun* cafeteria, canteen	
โรง rohng	*Noun* building	'โรง' (rohng) by itself means 'building.' Though Thai never used 'โรง' (rohng) as a stand alone word, we always combine with other word to form a specific type of buildings. These are common words begin with 'โรง' (rohng): - โรงเรียน (rohng-riian): school - โรงแรม (rohng raem): hotel - โรงพยาบาล (rohng-pá-yaa-baan): hospital - โรงงาน (rohng-ngaan): factory - โรงหนัง (rohng-năng): cinema
กัน gan	*Personal Pronoun* 1. one another, each other *Adverb* 2. together, jointly *Verb* 3. [to] keep out, prevent, set aside	
หลาย lăai	*Quantifier* many, several	

คำศัพท์ Vocabulary

Vocabulary	Definition	Note
หลายอย่าง lǎai-yàang	*Adjective* varied, numerous, many	
ว่า wâa	*Conjunction* 1. that *Verb* 2. [to] say, tell *Verb* 3. [to] blame, criticise	
Food Court Food court	*Noun* food court	
ห้าง hâang	*Noun* department store	
 **ขี้เกียจ** kêe-gìiat	*Stative Verb; Adjective* [to be] lazy	
ขี้ kêe	*Noun* 1. excrement, waste, residue *Prefix* 2. UNTRANSLATABLE We can't translate this meaning into a direct English equivalent. It's a prefix that indicates the following adjective is a quality of the person being referred to.	These are common combined words begin with ขี้ (kêe): - ขี้เล่น (kêe-lên): [to be] playful - ขี้เหงา (kêe-ngǎo): [to be] lonely - ขี้เมา (kêe-mao): [to be] alcoholic - ขี้อาย (kêe-aai): [to be] shy

คำศัพท์ Vocabulary

Vocabulary	Definition	Note
ร้านอาหารตามสั่ง ráan-aa-hăan-dtaam-sàng	*Noun* made-to-order restaurant	
สั่ง sàng	*Verb* [to] order, command, direct	
ตาม dtaam	*Preposition* 1. along, around, among, through *Verb* 2. [to] follow, pursue, come after *Preposition* 3. according to, in accordance with	
หน้าปากซอย nâa-bpàak-soi	*Combined words* entrance to the side street	
ซอย soi	*Noun* 1. a side-street off a main road *Verb* 2. [to] slice, mince, divide	
แวะ wáe	*Verb* [to] stop by, call at, call on	
 น้ำปั่น náam-bpàn	*Noun* smoothie	

คำศัพท์ Vocabulary

Vocabulary	Definition	Note
 ปั่น bpàn	*Verb* [to] spin, blend	
ร้าน ráan	*Noun* shop, store, booth	
ข้าง ๆ kâang-kâang	*Preposition* by, at the side of, near, next to	
เมื่อกี้ mêuua-gêe	*Adverb* just now, a moment ago	

Exercise 1 Listen to Thai sentences from your teacher and select the picture according to the sentence.
ฟังคุณครูพูดภาษาไทยและเลือกรูปภาพที่สอดคล้องกับประโยคที่คุณครูพูด

1. ฉันลดความอ้วนอยู่

A

B

C

2. โรงอาหารมีอาหารให้เลือกหลายอย่าง

A

B

C

3. Food court ในห้างมีแอร์เย็น ๆ

A

B

C

4. ผมอยากกินข้าวมันไก่

5. Food court อยู่ไกล ฉันขี้เกียจเดิน

Exercise 2

Translate these sentences into Thai.
แปลประโยคต่อไปนี้เป็นภาษาไทย

1. Shall we go eat Thai BBQ next week?

....

2. I don't like Tom Yum because it's too sour.

....

3. The hotel is far; you have to take a motorcycle taxi.

....

4. The chicken rice shop is next to Sandy's Coffee Shop.

....

5. This restaurant is good because it has many foods to choose.

....

Grammar 1

ไปกินข้าวมันไก่กัน

Bpai gin kâao-man-gài gan

(Let's) Go to eat Hainanese chicken rice together.

Structure: sentence + กัน (gan)

Explanation: 'กัน' (gan) is an adverb used at the end of the sentence – which involved more than one person doing something to each other; or together (jointly or alongside).

'กัน' (gan) can be used in various situations to give different meanings, the most common uses are:

1. 'กัน' (gan) as 'each other'. For example, พวกเราโกรธกัน (Pûuak-rao gròht gan) means 'we are angry at each other'.

2. 'กัน' (gan) as an invitation to do something together just like 'let's' in English. For example, ไปกัน (Bpai-gan) means 'Let's go!'

3. 'ด้วยกัน' (dûuay-gan) as 'together'. For example, พวกเราไปด้วยกัน (Pûuak-rao bpai dûuay-gan) means 'we go together'.

4. เหมือนกัน (mĕuuan-gan) as alike or same as one another. For example, พวกเราแต่งตัวเหมือนกัน (Pûuak-rao dtàeng-dtuua mĕuuan-gan) means 'we dress alike'.

For example:

1. 1. พวกเขารักกัน
   Pûuak-kăo rák gan
   They love each other.

2. พวกเขาไม่รักกัน
   Pûuak-kăo mâi-rák gan
   They don't love each other.

3. พรุ่งนี้ทำงานกัน
   Prûng-née tam-ngaan gan
   Let's work tomorrow.

4. พวกเราทำงานด้วยกัน
   Pûuak-rao tam-ngaan dûuay-gan
   We work together.

5. งานของพวกเราเหมือนกัน
   Ngaan kŏng-pûuak-rao mĕuuan-gan
   Our works are the same.

Exercise 1 Read Thai sentences and translate them into English.
อ่านประโยคภาษาไทยและแปลเป็นภาษาอังกฤษ

1.) หมา 2 ตัวสู้กัน
Măa-sŏng-dtuua sôo gan

....

2.) ไปเที่ยวจตุจักรกัน
Bpai-tîieow jà-dtù-jàk gan

....

3.) ไปเที่ยวจตุจักรกันมั้ย
Bpai-tîieow jà-dtù-jàk gan mái

....

4.) พวกเราไปเที่ยวจตุจักรด้วยกัน
Pûuak-rao bpai-tîieow jà-dtù-jàk dûuay-gan

....

5.) พวกเราไม่เคยไปจตุจักรเหมือนกัน
Pûuak-rao mâi-koiie-bpai jà-dtù-jàk mĕuuan-gan

....

Exercise 2 Say these sentences in Thai.
พูดประโยคต่อไปนี้เป็นภาษาไทย

1. Haven't met each other for long time.
(Hint: Long time no see – from chapter 1)

2. (Let's) See you tomorrow.

3. (Let's) Go on diet.

4. Yesterday we had a meeting together.

5. We are busy, same as one another.

TSL4U

Grammar 2

แอร์เย็นด้วย

Ae yen dûuay

Air conditioner is cold also.

Structure and Explanation:

ด้วย (dûuay) has 3 meanings:

1. If putting in front of nouns, it means 'by, with, through'. This is a formal language; you may not hear in everyday conversation much. For example:
   (1) ผมเรียนภาษาไทยด้วยตัวเอง
   Pŏm riian paa-săa-tai dûuay-dtuua-eng
   I study Thai language by myself.
   (2) ของฝากชิ้นนี้ทำด้วยมือ
   Kŏng-fàak chín-née tam-dûuay-meu
   This souvenir is made by hand.
   (3) เดินทางด้วยเรือ 2 วันและรถไฟ 2 วัน
   Dern-taang dûuay reuua song-wan láe rót-fai song-wan
   Travel by cruise 2 days and by train 2 days.

2. If combining with 'กัน' (gan); ด้วยกัน (dûuay-gan) means 'to do something together' as we already explained in last grammar point.

3. If putting the end of sentences, it means 'also, as well, too'. This is the most common structure used in everyday conversation and our exercises will focus on this structure.

For example:

1. เอาอันนี้ อันนั้น และอันโน้นด้วย
Ao an-née an-nán láe an-nóhn dûuay
I take this one, that one and that further one too.

2. เรียนภาษาไทยง่ายและสนุกด้วย
Riian paa-săa-tai ngâai láe sà-nùk dûuay
Learning Thai language is easy and fun.

3. เมื่อวานแม่ไม่ได้ไปด้วย
Mêuua-waan mâe mâi-dâai-bpai-dûuay
Yesterday mum didn't go (with us).
NOTE: ไม่ได้ (mâi dâai) + verb is a structure for past simple tense.

4. พรุ่งนี้แม่จะไปด้วย
Prûng-née mâe jà-bpai-dûuay
Tomorrow mum will go (with us).

5. ฉันขอนั่งด้วยได้มั้ย
Chăn-kŏr nâng-dûuay dâai-mái
May I sit with you?

Exercise 1

Read Thai sentences and translate them into English.
อ่านประโยคภาษาไทยและแปลเป็นภาษาอังกฤษ

1.) ร้านนี้รับเงินสด สแกน และบัตรเครดิตด้วย
Ráan-née ráp ngern-sòt scan láe bàt-kray-dìt dûuay

....

2.) อาหารร้านนี้อร่อยและไม่แพงด้วย
Aa-hăan ráan-née à-ròi láe mâi-paeng dûuay

....

3.) ไปกินข้าวแล้วก็ดูหนังด้วย
Bpai gin-kâao láew-gôr doo-năng dûuay

....

4.) ขอซื้อป๊อปคอร์นด้วยได้มั้ย
Kŏr séu popcorn dûuay dâai-mái

....

5.) ทำไมต้องกินป๊อปคอร์นด้วย
Tam-mai dtông-gin popcorn dûuay

....

Exercise 2

Say these sentences in Thai.
พูดประโยคต่อไปนี้เป็นภาษาไทย

1. This restaurant has promotion too.
2. Buy clothes, hat, and glasses too.
3. I want to watch movie too.
4. Do you want popcorn as well?
5. May I have Coke as well?

Grammar 3

ฉันลดความอ้วนอยู่

Chăn lót-kwaam-ûuan yòo

I am in process of losing weight (I am on diet now).

Structure and Explanation:

There are 3 structures to form present continuous tense. Each structure gives slightly different feelings in various situations; however, they can be used interchangeably in most situations.

1. sentence + อยู่ (yòo)

'อยู่' (yòo) as a verb means 'being at' usually followed by a location. For example, ฉันอยู่บ้าน (Chăn-yòo-bâan) means 'I am at home'.

However, 'อยู่' (yòo) can also be a helping verb (secondary verb) to put at the end of the sentence - to form the present continuous tense. 'อยู่' (yòo) in this case indicates that the verb in that particular sentence is happening at the present moment. For example, ฉันกินข้าวอยู่ (Chăn gin-kâao yòo) means 'I am eating (at the present moment)'.

2. กำลัง (gam-lang) + Verb

'กำลัง' (gam-lang) is similar to 'อยู่' (yòo); it is a helping verb (secondary verb) – to put in front of the main verb to emphasize that the particular verb (action) is in process of happening. Therefore, it is another form of present continuous tense. For example, ฉันกำลังกินข้าว (Chăn gam-lang gin-kâao) means 'I am in process of eating'.

3. กำลัง (gam-lang) + Verb + อยู่ (yòo)

Both 'กำลัง' (gam-lang) and 'อยู่' (yòo) are helping verbs to form present continuous tense. They can be used interchangeably and/or even used together in one sentence. For example, ฉันกำลังกินข้าวอยู่ (Chăn gam-lang gin-kâao yòo) means 'I am in process of eating, at the present moment'.

For example:

1. แม่ทำอาหารอยู่
Mâe tam-aa-hăan yòo
Mum is cooking at the present moment.

2. แม่กำลังทำอาหาร
Mâe gam-lang tam aa-hăan
Mum is in process of cooking.

3. แม่กำลังทำอาหารอยู่
Mâe gam-lang tam aa-hăan yòo
Mum is in process of cooking at the present moment.

4. แม่ทำอะไรอยู่
Mâe tam-à-rai yòo
What is mum doing, at the present moment?

5. แม่กำลังทำอะไร
Mâe gam-lang tam-à-rai
What is mum in process of doing?

6. แม่กำลังทำอะไรอยู่
Mâe gam-lang tam-à-rai yòo
What is mum in process of doing, at the present moment?

Exercise 1

Read Thai sentences and translate them into English.
อ่านประโยคภาษาไทยและแปลเป็นภาษาอังกฤษ

1.) ผมประชุมอยู่
Pŏm bprà-chum yòo

....

2.) เพื่อนกำลังดูหนัง
Pêuuan gam-lang doo-năng

....

3.) คุณกำลังกินอะไร
Kun gam-lang gin-à-rai

....

4.) ฉันกับเพื่อนกินหมูกระทะกันอยู่
Chăn gàp pêuuan gin mŏo-grà-tá gan yòo

....

5.) คุณกำลังยุ่งอยู่มั้ย
Kun gam-lang yûng yòo mái

....

Exercise 2

Say these sentences in Thai.
พูดประโยคต่อไปนี้เป็นภาษาไทย

1. Where are they going?
2. They are going to department store.
3. We are walking to made-to-order restaurant.
4. Who is on diet?
5. Whom are you eating Hainanese chicken rice with?

Fun Fact:

'ขี้เกียจ' (kêe-giiat) literally means 'to be lazy' but for spoken language, sometimes you may hear Thai people use it instead of 'do not want to do that particular action'. For example, when Jane says "ขี้เกียจเดิน" (kêe-giiat-dern), she actually means "I don't want to walk".

More examples are:

1. ขี้เกียจกิน
   Kêe-giiat-gin
   Don't want to eat.

2. ขี้เกียจเจอคนเยอะ ๆ
   Kêe-giiat-jer kon-yúh-yúh
   Don't want to meet many people.

3. ขี้เกียจฟังแม่บ่น
   Kêe-giiat-fang mâe bòn
   Don't want to listen to mum complaining.

Challenge: Do you have anything that you are too lazy to even imagine doing it?

" "

Chapter 9

ยินดีให้บริการ

Yin-dee-hâi-bor-rí-gaan

Pleasure to serve you.

พอลโทรไปเช่ารถ Paul toh bpai châo-rót

1 ยินดีเลยค่ะคุณลูกค้า ทางเราขอมัดจำตอนนี้ 50%
และจ่ายอีก 50% ตอนมารับรถที่แอร์พอร์ต
คุณลูกค้าสะดวกมั้ยคะ
Yin-dee-loiie kâ kun-lôok-káa
Taang-rao kŏr mát-jam dton-née hâa-sìp-percent
Láe jàai-èek hâa-sìp-percent
dton-maa-ráp-rót têe airport
Kun-lôok-káa sà-dùuak-mai ká
2 สะดวกครับ
Sà-dùuak kráp

1 หทัยชนกได้ทำการจองรถ
ให้คุณลูกค้าเรียบร้อยแล้ว
Hà-tai-chá-nók
dâai-tam-gaan-jong-rót-
hâi-kun-lôok-káa-rîiap-rói-láew
2 ทางเราจะส่งอีเมลเพื่อคอนเฟิร์มอีกครั้ง
ถ้าคุณลูกค้าไม่ได้รับอีเมลภายใน 5 นาทีหลังจากนี้
กรุณาติดต่อกลับมาอีกครั้งนะคะ
Taang-rao jà song-email
pêuua-confirm-èek-kráng
Tâa kun-lôok-káa mâi-dâai-ráp-email
paai-nai-hâa-naa-tee lăng-jàak-née
Gà-rú-naa-dtìt-dtòr-glàp-maa-èek-kráng ná-ká
3 ได้ครับ ขอบคุณครับ
Dâai kráp Kòp-kun kráp

English Translation

Paul calls for a car rental.

Call Center : Hello. This is Phuket Cars Rental. Hataichanok is glad to service you.

Paul : Hello. I'd like to rent a 7-seater car next Friday.

Call Center : Definitely.
How many days will you come to Phuket?
(How long will you stay in Phuket?)

Paul : 4 day, please.
I will return the car on Monday evening.

Call Center : With pleasure, sir. We would require 50% deposit for now.
And another 50% when you pick up the car at the airport.
Is it convenient for you?

Paul : Yes, it is.

Call Center : Hathaichanok booked the car for you already.

Call Center : We will sent email for confirmation once more time.
If you don't (get to) receive the email within the next 5 minutes after this, please kindly get back to us once again.

Paul : Sure. Thank you.

คำศัพท์ Vocabulary

Vocabulary	Definition	Note
 โทร toh	*Verb* [to] call, telephone, phone	
 ยินดี yin-dee	*Stative Verb; Adjective* [to be] happy, glad	
บริการ bor-rí-gaan	*Noun* service	
เช่ารถ châo-rót	*Combined words* [to] rent a car	
เช่า châo	*Verb* [to] rent, hire, lease	
 รถ rót	*Noun* car, vehicle	
ที่นั่ง têe-nâng	*Noun* seat, place	

คำศัพท์ Vocabulary

Vocabulary	Definition	Note
วันศุกร์หน้า wan-sùk-nâa	*Combined words* next Friday	
ลูกค้า lôok káa	*Noun* customer, client	Fun fact: 'ลูก' (lôok) by itself means child or offspring; and 'ค้า' (káa) means [to] trade or to do business. Putting the two words together 'ลูกค้า' (lôok-káa) means customer or client. Guess how to call the seller, or merchant in Thai? It is 'แม่ค้า' (mâe-káa) for female seller(s) and 'พ่อค้า' (pôr-káa) for male seller(s)
คุณลูกค้า kun-lôok-káa	*Combined words* precious customers; this is very common way for sellers and companies to address/refer to their customer(s).	
คืน keun	*Noun* 1. night *Verb* 2. [to] return, restore	
ทางเรา taang-rao	*Combined words* our way; this is a sometimes-used word for sellers and companies to address/refer to themselves.	
มัดจำ mát-jam	*Verb* 1. [to] deposit *Noun* 2. deposit, down payment	

คำศัพท์ Vocabulary

Vocabulary	Definition	Note
% เปอร์เซ็นต์ percent	*Noun* percent, percentage	
ตอน dton	*Preposition* 1. when, during, at *Noun* 2. section, piece, bit, part, episode	
 แอร์พอร์ต airport	*Noun* airport	Airport in Thai is 'สนามบิน' (sà-năam-bin), which we have already learnt in chapter one. Though many people will use 'airport' instead.
สะดวก sà-dùuak	*Adverb* 1. conveniently, comfortably, smoothly *Verb* 2. [to be] convenient, comfortable	
 จอง jong	*Verb* [to] reserve, book, hold	
การ gaan	*Prefix* UNTRANSLATABLE We can't translate this meaning into a direct English equivalent. It's a prefix which converts a verb or adjective into a verbal noun. For example: - การเรียน (gaan-riian): education - การงาน (gaan-ngaan): career, profession - การเมือง (gaan-meuuang): politics	Recap from chapter 8: 'ความ' (kwaam) is a prefix which converts a verb or an adjective into an abstract noun. For example: ความรู้ (kwaam-róo): knowledge ความคิด (kwaam-kít): thoughts, idea ความสามารถ (kwaam-săa-mâat): ability, talent ความจริง (kwaam-jing): truth ความร้อน (kwaam-rón): heat ความรู้สึก (kwaam-róo-sèuk): feeling ความสวย (kwaam-sŭuay): beauty

คำศัพท์ Vocabulary

Vocabulary	Definition	Note
ทำการจอง tam-gaan-jong	*Combined words* [to do the action of] booking	
เรียบร้อย rîiap-rói	*Verb* 1. [to be] ready, set 2. [to be] polite, well-mannered	
ส่ง sòng	*Verb* [to] send	
 **อีเมล** e-mail	*Noun* e-mail	
เพื่อ pêuua	*Conjunction* for, in order to	
คอนเฟิร์ม confirm	*Verb* [to] confirm	

คำศัพท์ Vocabulary

Vocabulary	Definition	Note
ครั้ง kráng	*Noun* time, occasion	
ภายใน paai-nai	*Adverb* 1. inside, interior, internal 2. within	
หลัง lăng	*Adjective* 1. following, next, later *Preposition* 2. after, behind *Adjective; Adverb* 3. back, behind, rear	
หลังจากนี้ lăng-jàak-née	*Conjunction* after, afterwards, later, next	
กรุณา gà-rú-naa	*Adverb* please, kindly	
ติดต่อ dtìt-dtòr	*Verb* [to] contact, make contact with, communicate	
กลับ glàp	*Verb* to] return, go back, reverse	

Phrase

Phrase	Definition	Note
ยินดีให้บริการ Yin-dee-hâi-bor-rí-gaan	Glad to be of service.	
ยินดีเลย (ค่ะ/ครับ) Yin-dee-loiie (kâ/kráp)	You are very welcome.	
กรุณาติดต่อกลับ Gà-rú-naa-dtìt-dtòr-glàp	Please kindly get back to me/us.	

Exercise 1

Choose the correct sentence to complete the conversation.
เลือกประโยคที่ทำให้บทสนทนาสมบูรณ์

พนักงาน: สวัสดีค่ะ Phuket Seafood ยินดีให้บริการค่ะ Pá-nák-ngaan : Sà-wàt-dee kâ Phuket Seafood yin-dee hâi-bor-rí-gaan kâ พอล: .... Paul:	A. สวัสดีครับ ผมขอจองโต๊ะวันเสาร์นี้ 5 โมงเย็น Sà-wàt-dee kráp Pŏm kŏr-jong-dtó wan-săo-née hâa-mohng-yen B. สวัสดีครับ ผมขอจองรถวันเสาร์นี้ 5 โมงเย็น Sà-wàt-dee kráp Pŏm kŏr-jong-rót wan-săo-née hâa-mohng-yen
พนักงาน: .... Pá-nák-ngaan : .... พอล: ทั้งหมด 6 คนครับ Paul: Táng-mòt-hòk-kon kráp	A. คุณลูกค้าจะมากี่คนคะ Kun-lôok-káa jà maa-gèe-kon ká B. คุณลูกค้าจะมากี่โมงคะ Kun-lôok-káa jà maa-gèe-mohng ká
พนักงาน: ขอ .... ของคุณลูกค้าด้วยค่ะ Pá-nák-ngaan : Kŏr .... kŏng kun-lôok-káa dûuay kâ พอล: พอล 066-678-6789 ครับ Paul: Paul Sŏon-hòk-hòk hòk-jèt-bpàet hòk-jèt-bpàet-gâo kráp	A. ชื่อกับอีเมล chêu gàp email B. ชื่อกับเบอร์โทร chêu gàp ber-toh

พนักงาน: .... Pá-nák-ngaan : .... พอล: ขอเป็นข้างในดีกว่าครับ Paul: Kŏr bpen kâang-nai dee-gwàa kráp	A. คุณลูกค้าจะนั่งข้างนอกหรือข้างในดีคะ Kun-lôok-káa jà nâng-kâang-nôk-rĕu-kâang-nai-dee ká B. คุณลูกค้าจะสั่งอาหารเลยมั้ยคะ Kun-lôok-káa jà sàng-aa-hăan-loiie-mái ká

พนักงาน: ....โต๊ะข้างในมีคนจองหมดแล้วค่ะ Pá-nák-ngaan : ....dtó kâang-nai mee-kon-jong-mòt-láew kâ พอล: งั้นเป็นโต๊ะข้างนอก ใกล้ทะเลก็ได้ครับ Paul: Ngán-bpen dtó-kâang-nôk glâi-tá-lay gôr-dâai kráp	A. ขอโทษค่ะ Kŏr-tôht kâ B. เรียบร้อยแล้วค่ะ Rîiap-rói-láew kâ

Exercise 2

Put these words in the correct order.
เรียงคำให้เป็นประโยคที่ถูกต้อง

1. ผม เช่า บ้าน ขอ 3 เดือน
pŏm châo bâan kŏr săam deuuan

....

2. คุณลูกค้า มา เมื่อไหร่ จะ คะ
kun-lôok-káa maa mêuua-rài jà ká

....

3. ตอนนี้ 50% มัดจำ ค่ะ ขอ
dton-née hâa-sìp-percent mát-jam kâ kŏr

....

4. เงิน ยังไง จ่าย บ้าง ได้
ngern yang-ngai jàai bâang dâai

....

1. จอง แคนเซิล ไม่ได้ นะคะ แล้ว
jong cancel mâi-dâai ná-ká láew

....

Grammar 1

วันศุกร์หน้า

Wan-sùk nâa

Next Friday

Structure: time word + หน้า (nâa)

Explanation:

'หน้า' (nâa) has 4 meanings:

Definition	Word type	Example
1. Face	Noun	แต่งหน้า (dtàeng-nâa) Make up
2. Page	Noun and classifier	เปิดหน้า 20 (bpèrt nâa yêe-sìp) Open page 20. หนังสือมี 100 หน้า (năng-sěu mee nèung-rói nâa) The book has 100 pages.
3. In front of	Preposition	หน้าออฟฟิศ (nâa office) In front of the office
4. Next, following, upcoming	Adjective	วันศุกร์หน้า (wan-sùk-nâa) Next Friday

'หน้า' (nâa) in this chapter is working as an 'adjective' to give specification to Friday that is coming next week. The time word that can be combined with 'หน้า' (nâa) are including (but not limited to):

- Day: วันศุกร์หน้า (wan-sùk-nâa) Next Friday
- Week: สัปดาห์หน้า (sàp-daa-nâa) Next week
- Month: เดือนหน้า (deuuan-nâa) Next month
- Season: ฤดูหน้า (réu-doo-nâa) Next season
- Time: ครั้งหน้า (kráng-nâa) Next time

Additional note 1: The 'adjective' to make time word 'present' in the same way as 'this' in English is 'นี้' (née). For example:

- Day: วันศุกร์นี้ (wan-sùk-née) This Friday
- Week: สัปดาห์นี้ (sàp-daa-née) This week
- Month: เดือนนี้ (deuuan-née) This month
- Season: ฤดูนี้ (réu-doo-née) This season
- Time: ครั้งนี้ (kráng-née) This time

Additional note 2: The 'adjective' that indicates that the 'time' has already passed, in the same way as 'last' in English is ที่แล้ว (têe-láew). For example:

- Day: วันศุกร์ที่แล้ว (wan-sùk têe-láew) Last Friday
- Week: สัปดาห์ที่แล้ว (sàp-daa têe-láew) Last week
- Month: เดือนที่แล้ว (deuuan têe-láew) Last month
- Season: ฤดูที่แล้ว (réu-doo têe-láew) Last season
- Time: ครั้งที่แล้ว (kráng têe láew) Last time

In summary, the adjective that gives specification to time words are: (1) หน้า (nâa) next (2) นี้ (née) this and (3) ที่แล้ว (têe-láew) last.

For example:

1. วันจันทร์นี้พวกเราไปทำงาน
Wan-jan-née pûuak-rao bpai-tam-ngaan
This Monday, we go to work.

2. เดือนนี้เขาไม่ไปทำงาน
Deuuan-née kǎo mâi-bpai-tam-ngaan
This month, he doesn't go to work.

3. สัปดาห์หน้างานคุณ(จะ)ยุ่งมั้ย
Sàp-daa-nâa ngaan-kun (jà) yûng mái
Next week, (will) your work be busy?

4. อาทิตย์หน้างานผม(จะ)ไม่ยุ่ง
Aa-tít-nâa ngaan-ǒm (jà) mâi-yûng
Next week, my work (will) not be busy.

5. ครั้งที่แล้วเราประชุมกันกี่ชั่วโมง
Kráng-têe-láew rao bprà-chum-gan gèe-chûua-mohng
Last time, how many hours (did) we (have) a meeting together?

Exercise 1

Read Thai sentences and translate them into English.
อ่านประโยคภาษาไทยและแปลเป็นภาษาอังกฤษ

1.) ฤดูร้อนที่แล้วผมอยู่ที่ภูเก็ต
Réu-doo-rón têe-láew pŏm yòo têe poo-gèt

....

2.) ฤดูหนาวนี้เราจะไปเที่ยวที่ไหนกันดี
Réu-doo-nǎao-née rao jà-bpai-tîieow têe-nǎi gan dee

....

3.) ปีที่แล้วผมไปเชียงใหม่
Bpee-têe-láew pŏm bpai chiiang-mài

....

4.) ปีนี้คุณอยากไปเชียงใหม่กับผมมั้ย
Bpee-née kun yàak-bpai chiiang-mài gàp pŏm mái

....

5.) ผมอยากไปเชียงใหม่ปีหน้า
Pŏm yàak-bpai chiiang-mài bpee-nâa

....

Exercise 2

Say these sentences in Thai.
พูดประโยคต่อไปนี้เป็นภาษาไทย

1. I will go to Thailand next year.
2. I have studied Thai language since last month.
3. Last time, we learned number and price.
4. This time, what are we going to learn?
5. Next time, can we learn Thai food?

Grammar 2

วันจันทร์ตอนเย็น
Wan-jan dton-yen
Monday evening

Structure: ตอน (dton) + time or event

Explanation and Example:

'ตอน' (dton) as a noun means 'section, part, episode'. For example, ซีรีส์เรื่องนี้มี 12 ตอน (series-rêuuang-née mee sìp-sǒng-dton) means 'this series has 12 episodes'.

'ตอน' (dton) as a preposition means 'when, during, at.' It can be followed by time or an event. Examples of 'ตอน' (dton) uses are including but not limited to:

Time

- ตอนเช้า (dton-cháo) in the morning
- ตอนเที่ยง (dton-tîiang) at noon
- ตอนบ่าย (dton-bàai) in the afternoon
- ตอนเย็น (dton-yen) in the evening
- ตอนกลางวัน (dton-glaang-wan) during the day
- ตอนกลางคืน (dton-glaang-keun) during the night

Question

- ตอนไหน (dton-nǎi) when?

Adverb

- ตอนนี้ (dton-née) at this time (now)
- ตอนนั้น (dton-nán) at that time

Event

- ตอนผมเป็นเด็ก (dton-pǒm-bpen-dèk) when I was young.
- ตอนผมอยู่ที่เมืองไทย (dton-pǒm-yòo-têe-meuuang-tai) when I was in Thailand.
- ตอนดูหนัง (dton-doo-nǎng) when watching movie.
- ตอนกินข้าว (dton-gin-kâao) when eating.

Exercise 1

Read Thai sentences and translate them into English.
อ่านประโยคภาษาไทยและแปลเป็นภาษาอังกฤษ

1.) ตอนอยู่กับคุณ ผมมีความสุข
Dton-yòo-gàp-kun pŏm-mee-kwaam-sùk

....

2.) ตอนอยู่กับผม คุณรู้สึกยังไง
Dton-yòo-gàp-pŏm kun-róo-sèuk-yang-ngai

....

3.) ตอนคุณเหงา คุณทำอะไร
Dton-kun-ngăo kun-tam-à-rai

....

4.) ตอนนี้ผมไม่มีใคร
Dton-née pŏm-mâi-mee-krai

....

5.) ผมอยากเจอคุณตอนเช้าของทุกวัน
Pŏm-yàak-jer-kun dton-cháo-kŏng-túk-wan

....

Exercise 2

Say these sentences in Thai.
พูดประโยคต่อไปนี้เป็นภาษาไทย

1. I work in the morning.
2. I don't watch series at night.
3. I like to watch series when eating.
4. When do you like to watch series?
5. Now, do you want to watch series together?

TSL4U

Grammar 3

ได้จองรถแล้ว

Dâai jong rót láew

Booked the car already. (The car has been booked).

(หทัยชนกได้ทำการจองรถให้คุณลูกค้าเรียบร้อยแล้ว)
Hà-tai-chá-nók dâai-tam-gaan-jong-rót hâi kun-lôok-káa rîiap-rói láew
Hathaichanok booked the car for you (valued customer) already.

Structure: dâai + verb + láew

Explanation:

'ได้' (dâai) has 3 uses:

(1) as a verb means 'to get, receive, obtain'; often comes in structure: ได้ (dâai) + noun. For example, ได้รถใหม่ (dâai-rót-mài) Get a new car.

(2) as a secondary verb means 'can, to be able to'; often comes in structure: verb + ได้ (dâai). For example, ขับรถได้ (kàp-rót-dâai) Can drive a car.

(3) as a helping verb (adverb auxiliary) means 'got to, get to, did'; often comes in structure: ได้ (dâai) + verb. For example, ได้ขับรถ (dâai-kàp-rót) Get to drive a car (drove a car).

Note: the usage number 1 is straightforward; usage number 2 has been taught in chapter 3. This chapter we will focus on usage number 3.

'แล้ว' (láew) is an adverb meaning 'already'. It can be used to form past sentences simply by putting after the verb or at the end of the sentences. For example, 'จองรถแล้ว' (jong-rót-láew) which means 'booked the car already'.

Please note, both 'ได้' (dâai) and 'แล้ว' (láew) indicates that the sentences are in the past – or already happened.

For statement, they can be used together or separately as structures below:

1. ได้ (dâai)+ verb + แล้ว (láew)
2. ได้ (dâai) + verb
3. verb + แล้ว (láew)

For example:

1. พอลได้ไปตลาดนัดจตุจักรแล้ว
Paul dâai bpai dtà-làat-nát jà-dtù-jàk láew
Paul got to go to Chatuchak market already.

2. พอลได้ไปตลาดนัดจตุจักร
Paul dâai bpai dtà-làat-nát jà-dtù-jàk
Paul got to go to Chatuchak market.

3. พอลไปตลาดนัดจตุจักรแล้ว
Paul bpai dtà-làat-nát jà-dtù-jàk láew
Paul went to Chatuchak market already.

For negative sentences, it is used in this structure only: ไม่ได้ (mâi-dâai) + verb

For example:

พอลไม่ได้ไปตลาดนัดจตุจักร
Paul mâi dâai bpai dtà-làat-nát jà-dtù-jàk
Paul didn't get to go to Chatuchak market.

For closed questions, it is used in this structure only: ได้ (dâai) + verb + มั้ย (mái)

For example:

พอลได้ไปตลาดนัดจตุจักรมั้ย
Paul dâai bpai dtà-làat-nát jà-dtù-jàk mái
Did Paul get to go to Chatuchak market?

Exercise 1

Read Thai sentences and translate them into English.
อ่านประโยคภาษาไทยและแปลเป็นภาษาอังกฤษ

1.) ผมซื้อของฝากแล้ว
Pŏm séu kŏng-fàak láew

....

2.) พวกเขาไม่ได้ซื้อของฝาก
Pûuak-kăo mâi-dâai-séu kŏng-fàak

....

3.) พวกคุณได้ซื้อของฝากจากกาญจนบุรีมั้ย
Pûuak-kun dâai-séu kŏng-fàak jàak gaan-jà-ná-bù-ree mái

....

4.) ใครได้รับของฝากแล้วบ้าง
Krai dâai-ráp kŏng-fàak láew bâang

....

5.) คุณได้รับของฝากเมื่อไหร่
Kun dâai-ráp kŏng-fàak mêuua-rài

....

Exercise 2

Say these sentences in Thai – using your preferred structures.
พูดประโยคต่อไปนี้เป็นภาษาไทย - โดยเลือกโครงสร้างประโยคที่นักเรียนถนัด

1. I drank coffee already.
2. We got to eat Shabu together last month.
3. I didn't get to study Thai language yesterday.
4. Last time, did you get to eat Moograta?
5. Which market did you go already?

Fun Fact:

Traffic laws in Thailand are often loosely enforced, with many drivers ignoring speed limits, traffic signals, and other regulations.

Challenge: Discuss with your teacher about the differences between Thailand's traffice laws and those of your country.

Chapter 10

ดีเลยครับ

Dee-loiie kráp

That's great!

พอลเช็กอินที่โรงแรม Paul chék-in têe-rohng-raem

1 ทาร่าขออัปเกรดเป็นห้อง Grand Deluxe
วิวทะเล ชั้นบนสุดให้แทนได้มั้ยคะ
Taa-râa kŏr-upgrade bpen hông-grand deluxe
wiw-tá-lay chán-bon-sùt hâi-taen dâai-mái ká
2 ดีเลยครับ ขอบคุณมากครับ
Dee-loiie kráp
Kòp-kun-mâak kráp

1 นี่กุญแจกับ password Wi-Fi ค่ะ
Nêe gun-jae gàp password wifi kâ
2 อาหารเช้าเริ่ม 6 โมงถึง 11 โมงเช้า
Aa-hăan-cháo rêrm hòk-mohng-
tĕung-sìp-èt-mohng-cháo
3 ห้องอาหารอยู่ชั้น 2 เข้าไปทานได้เลยนะคะ
Hông-aa-hăan-yòo-chán-sŏng
Kâo-bpai-taan-dâai-loiie ná-ká
4 ขอบคุณมากครับ
Kòp-kun-mâak kráp

English Translation

Paul checks in at a hotel.

Receptionist : Welcome to Phuket Boutique Hotel.

Paul : We (have) booked for 3 room by booking.com

Receptionist : I'm glad to serve you. What name is the reservation under?
Could I have your passport or Thai ID card, please?

Paul : Here you are.

Receptionist : Er..... Customer, On behalf of the hotel, (we) must apologize.
Just exactly last night, it rained heavily and then the ceiling was leaked

Receptionist : The room in the zone you (have) booked, can not open for the service.

Receptionist : Can Tara (can I) upgrade the rooms for you to Grand Deluxe, sea view, on the top floor instead?
(Note : It is common in Thailand for people to refer to themselves by their name. In this story, Tara is of the receptionist.)

Paul : That's great. Thank you so much.

Receptionist : Here are (your) keys and Wi-Fi passwords.
Breakfast start 6 o'clock to 11 o'clock in the morning.
The dining room is on the second floor. (You) can get in to eat.

Paul : Thank you so much.

คำศัพท์ Vocabulary

Vocabulary	Definition	Note
 เช็กอิน check in	*Verb* [to] check in	
ไว้ wái	*Verb* [to] keep, save, store	
จองไว้ jong-wái	*Combined words* [to be] reserved, booked	
ผ่าน pàan	*Verb* [to] pass, pass over, pass by	
รบกวน róp-guuan	*Verb* 1. [to] annoy, bother 2. Will you please?	
 พาสปอร์ต passport	*Noun* passport	

คำศัพท์ Vocabulary

Vocabulary	Definition	Note
 บัตรประชาชน bàt-bprà-chaa-chon	*Noun* Thai ID card	
ประชาชน bprà-chaa-chon	*Noun* people, residents	
เอ่อ èr	*Interjection* erm, err, yeah	
พอดี por-dee	*Adverb* 1. exactly, just enough, just right *Adverb* 2. at the right moment, just then, just now	Fun fact: for clothes, Thais use 'พอดี' (por-dee) to describe something that fits; and we use 'ฟิต' (fit) to describe something that is too small.
เมื่อคืน mêuua-keun	*Noun* last night	
หนัก nàk	*Adverb* 1. severely, harshly *Stative Verb; Adjective* 2. [to be] heavy, hard 3. [to be] serious, severe	
 ฝนตกหนัก fǒn-dtòk-nàk	*Combined words* heavily raining	

TSL4U

คำศัพท์ Vocabulary

Vocabulary	Definition	Note
แล้ว láew	*Adverb* already *Conjunction* and, and then, and after that	
เพดาน pay-daan	*Noun* ceiling	
รั่ว rûua	*Verb* [to] leak, leak out	
โซน sohn	*Noun* zone, area	
สามารถ săa-mâat	*Adverb Auxiliary* can, be able to	
ให้บริการ hâi-bor-rí-gaan	*Verb* [to] service, provide service, serve	
อัปเกรด upgrade	*Verb* [to] upgrade	

คำศัพท์ Vocabulary

Vocabulary	Definition	Note
 วิวทะเล wiw-tá-lay	*Combined words* sea view	
วิว wiw	*Noun* view, landscape, panorama	
 ทะเล tá-lay	*Noun* sea, ocean	
ชั้นบนสุด chán-bon-sùt	*Combined words* top floor	
ชั้น chán	*Noun* 1. class, rank, grade 2. layer, level, stage 3. floor, storey (of a building) 4. rack, shelf	
สุด sùt	*Noun* 1. end, finish 2. maximum, peak, highest point *Verb* 3. [to] end, come to an end, finish *Secondary Verb* 4. most	

คำศัพท์ Vocabulary

Vocabulary	Definition	Note
แทน taen	*Conjunction* instead of	
 กุญแจ gun-jae	*Noun* key, lock	
password Wi-Fi password wifi	*Noun* Wi-Fi password	
ห้องอาหาร hông-aa-hăan	*Noun* dining room, eating room, restaurant	
อาหารเช้า aa-hăan-cháo	*Noun* breakfast	
เริ่ม rêrm	*Verb* [to] start, begin	
ทาน taan	*Verb* 1. [to] eat 2. [to] resist, oppose 3. [to] check up, re-read *Noun* 4. alms, gift, donation	'ทาน' (taan) is a formal way of saying 'eat'. This is not an everyday-conversation-word among friends; but you may come across when you are a customer and the seller(s)/ service provider(s) want to give you extra politeness.

Exercise 1 True or false.
ถูกหรือผิด

1.)..................... พอลจองที่พักไว้ 3 ห้อง
Paul jong-têe-pák-wái săam-hông

2.).....................เพดานรั่วเพราะฝนตก
Pay-daan-rûua prór-fŏn-dtòk

3.)..................... พอลกับเพื่อนได้อัปเกรดห้อง
Paul gàp pêuuan dâai-upgrade-hông

4.)..................... ที่โรงแรมไม่มี Wi-Fi
Têe-rohng-raem mâi-mee-wifi

5.)..................... อาหารเช้าเริ่ม 11 โมง
Aa-hăan-cháo rêrm sìp-èt-mohng

Exercise 2

Make sentences using these words.
แต่งประโยคจากคำที่กำหนด

1.) จอง (jong)

....

2.) เข้า (kâo)

....

3.) อัปเกรด (upgrade)

....

4.) แทน (taen)

....

5.) พอดี (por-dee) ขอ (kŏr)

....

Grammar 1

ผมจองไว้ 3 ห้อง

Pǒm-jong-wái-sǎam-hông

I booked for 3 rooms.

Structure, Explanation and Example:

"ไว้" (wái) is the commonly used word in Thai and has 3 meanings, as follows:

1 As a main verb meaning 'to keep, save, store'. It comes in structure ไว้ (wái) + noun. For example, (1) ไว้หนวด (wái-nùuat) to keep a moustache. (2) ไว้เครา (wái-krao) to keep a beard. (3) ไว้ผมยาว (wái-pǒm-yaao) to grow long hair.

2. As an adverb to make the main verb completed or stronger. It comes in structure verb +ไว้ (wái). For example, (1) เก็บไว้ (gèp-wái) to store safely (2) จองไว้ (jong-wái) to book successfully / to reserve (3) จำไว้ (jam-wái) to remember well/ to keep in mind.

3. As a helping verb to defer some actions or events to a future time. It comes in structure ไว้ (wái) + sentence. For example, (1) ไว้ครั้งหน้า (wái-kráng-nâa) keep it for next time. (2) ไว้ทีหลัง (wái-tee-lǎng) for later. (3) ไว้เจอกัน (wái-jer-gan) see you later.

TSL4U

Exercise 1

Read Thai sentences and translate them into English.
อ่านประโยคภาษาไทยและแปลเป็นภาษาอังกฤษ

1.) ผมชอบไว้หนวดตอนฤดูหนาว
Pŏm chôp wái-nùuat dton-réu-doo-năao

....

2.) ได้จองไว้มั้ย
Dâai-jong-wái mái

....

3.) จองไว้กี่วัน
Jong-wái gèe-wan

....

4.) คุณวางกุญแจไว้ที่ไหน
Kun waang gun-jae wái têe-năi

....

5.) พ่อวางกุญแจไว้ข้างๆ มือถือ
Pôr waang gun-jae wái kâang-kâang meu-tĕu

....

6.) ไว้เจอกันตอนผมไปเมืองไทย
Wái-jer-gan dton-pŏm-bpai-meuuang-tai

....

Exercise 2

Say these sentences in Thai – using your preferred structures.
พูดประโยคต่อไปนี้เป็นภาษาไทย - โดยเลือกโครงสร้างประโยคที่นักเรียนถนัด

1. I like to keep long hair.
2. My daughter doesn't like to keep long hair.
3. Who likes to keep long hair?
4. Mum puts mobile phone on the table.
4. Where does mum put mobile phone?
6. See you later.

Grammar 2

ทางโรงแรมต้องขอโทษด้วย

Taang-rohng-raem dtông-kǒr-tôht-dûuay

On behalf of the hotel, (we) must apologize.

Structure and Explanation:

'ทาง' (taang) by itself means 'way, path, route' when talking about locations or direction. For example, (1) ทางไหน (taang-nǎi) Which way? (2) ทางนี้ (taang-née) This way. (3) ทางนั้น (taang-nán) That way.

However, 'ทาง' (taang) can also be used as prefix meaning 'on behalf of one self' or 'from one's side' when putting in this structure: ทาง (taang) + noun. For example, (1) ทางเรา (taang-rao) From our side. (2) ทางโรงแรม (taang-rohng-raem) On behalf of the hotel. (3) ทางนี้ (taang-née) From this side.

Note: 'ทางนี้' (taang-née) can mean 'this way' or 'from our perspective' depending on the situation. This concept is also applied for 'ทางนั้น' (taang-nán) and 'ทางโน้น' (taang-nóhn).

For example:

1. ร้านอาหารไปทางไหน
   Ráan-aa-hǎan bpai taang-nǎi
   Which way is to go to the restaurant?

2. ร้านอาหารไปทางซ้าย
   Ráan-aa-hǎan bpai taang-sáai
   The restaurant is to the left.

3. โรงแรมอยู่ทางขวา
   Rohng-raem yòo taang-kwǎa
   The hotel is on the right side.

4. ทางโรงแรมมีอาหารเช้าให้
   Taang-rohng-raem mee aa-hǎan-cháo hâi
   The hotel provides breakfast.

5. ทางโรงแรมมีรถรับส่งมั้ย
   Taang-rohng-raem mee rót-ráp-sòng mái
   Does the hotel have shuttle bus?

Exercise 1 Read Thai sentences and translate them into English.
อ่านประโยคภาษาไทยและแปลเป็นภาษาอังกฤษ

1.) อโศกไปทางไหน
À-sòhk bpai taang-năi

....

2.) อโศกไปทางนั้น
À-sòhk bpai taang-nán

....

3.) ทำไมไม่ไปทางนี้
Tam-mai mâi-bpai taang-née

....

4.) ทางหัวหน้าจองรถให้แล้ว
Taang-hŭua-nâa jong-rót hâi-láew

....

5.) ทางหัวหน้าจองรถให้ใครบ้าง
Taang-hŭua-nâa jong-rót hâi-krai-bâang

....

Exercise 2 Say these sentences in Thai.
พูดประโยคต่อไปนี้เป็นภาษาไทย

1. Which way is to go to 7-11?
2. 7-11 can go many ways.
3. Which way do you want to go?
4. Does the hotel have a shuttle bus to go to 7-11?
5. The hotel has shuttle bus to the airport.

Grammar 3

พอดีเมื่อคืนฝนตกหนัก

Por-dee mêuua-keun fŏn-dtòk-nàk

Just exactly last night, it rained heavily.

Structure: พอดี (por-dee) + sentence
sentence + พอดี (por-dee)

Explanation and Example:

'พอดี' (por-dee) as an adjective means 'fit, enough, just right, exactly'. For example:

1. เสื้อตัวนี้พอดีกับคุณ
   Sêuua-dtuua-née por-dee gàp kun
   This shirt fits you just right.

2. ถ้วยเล็กเกินไป ใส่ก๋วยเตี๋ยวไม่พอดี
   Tûuay-lék-gern-bpai sài gŭuay-dtĭieow mâi-por-dee
   The bowl is too small, doesn't fit the noodle.

3. รองเท้าคู่นี้พอดีกับคุณมั้ย
   Rong-táo-kôo-née por-dee gàp-kun mái
   Does this pair of shoes fit you?

'พอดี' (por-dee) can also be an adverb, putting in front or after the sentence to emphasise that the sentence (or situation) has happened at that exact moment. This use of 'พอดี' (por-dee) can be for both expected or unexpected situations. For example:

1. เขามาพอดี
   Kăo-maa-por-dee
   Here he comes, just in time.

2. วันนี้ผมไม่เรียน พอดีครูไม่สบาย
   Wan-née pŏm-mâi-riian por-dee kroo-mâi-sà-baai
   Today I don't study, unexpectedly the teacher is unwell at the moment.

3. สิ้นเดือนเงินหมดพอดี
   Sîn-deuuan ngern-mòt por-dee
   End of the month, the money finished exactly / just enough.

Exercise 1

Read Thai sentences and translate them into English.
อ่านประโยคภาษาไทยและแปลเป็นภาษาอังกฤษ

1.) กระโปรงตัวใหญ่เกินไป ใส่ไม่พอดี
Grà-bprohng-dtuua-yài-gern-bpai sài-mâi-por-dee

....

2.) แล้วกางเกงล่ะ ใส่พอดีมั้ย
Láew-gaang-geng-lâ sài-por-dee-mái

....

3.) ดีใจที่ได้เจอคุณ ผมกำลังเหงาพอดี
Dee-jai-têe-dâai-jer-kun pŏm-gam-lang-ngăo-por-dee

....

4.) ผมกำลังหิวพอดี ไปกินหมูกระทะกันมั้ย
Pŏm-gam-lang-hĭw-por-dee bpai-gin-mŏo-grà-tá-gan-mái

....

5.) พอดีผมมีงานด่วน พวกคุณไปกันเลย
Por-dee-pŏm-mee-ngaan-dùuan pûuak-kun-bpai-gan-loiie

....

Exercise 2

Say these sentences in Thai.
พูดประโยคต่อไปนี้เป็นภาษาไทย

1. The hat is too small, doesn't fit you.
2. What about the glasses? Does it fit me?
3. I can't go to department store, at the moment I have meeting.
4. I can wait, at the moment I am not in hurry.
5. Or should we go tomorrow? The monthly salary will be out, just in time.

Fun fact:

1. Despite Thailand having 3 main seasons nationwide (summer, winter and raining seasons); the unique geography of southern Thailand is heavily influenced by monsoon winds, resulting in this region effectively experiencing only two distinct seasons - a rainy season and a hot season.

2. Phuket's rainy season spans from around May to October, with the heaviest rainfall typically occurring in September and October each year.

3. Phuket's tourism industry experiences distinct high and low seasons, with the hot seasons (November - April) drawing the most visitors, while the rainy season (May - October) sees fewer tourists.

Challenge: Role play with your classmate or teacher about the following scenario: you will go to Phuket on the 10-17th November with your friends. You will hire a car for 7 days. You need to explore different options and ask whether there is any promotion available.

Chapter 11

เอามาอย่างละหนึ่ง

Ao-maa-yàang-lá-nèung

(I will) take one each.

ที่ร้านอาหาร Têe ráan-aa-hăan

1
เมนูแนะนำที่นี่จะเป็นปูผัดผงกะหรี่
May-noo-náe-nam-têe-nêe-jà-bpen
bpoo-pàt-pŏng-gà-rèe
2
ข้าวผัดสับปะรด
kâao-pàt-sàp-bpà-rót
3
กุ้งราดซอสมะขาม
gûng-râat-sót-má-kăam
Phuket Seafood

1
หมึกทอดกระเทียม
Mèuk-tôt-grà-tiiam
2
ปลานึ่งมะนาว
bplaa-nêung-má-naao
3
แล้วก็ยำหอยแครงครับ
láew-gôr yam-hŏi-kraeng kráp
Phuket Seafood
4
เอามาอย่างละ 1 เลยค่ะ
Ao maa yàang-lá-nèung loiie kâ

English Translation

At a restaurant.

Paul	:	I want to eat clay pot roasted chicken.
Paul	:	Stir fried chicken with cashew nut.
Paul	:	And then stuffed omelette.
John	:	(We) come (to) Phuket then (we) must eat seafood.
Jay	:	Is there anything worth eating? Young brother (to call the waiter that looks younger) help recommending please.
Waiter	:	The recommended menus here are stir fried crab with curry powder.
Waiter	:	Pineapple fried rice.
Waiter	:	Crispy prawn in tamarind sauce.
Waiter	:	Crispy garlic calamari.
Waiter	:	Streamed fish with lime.
Waiter	:	And then spicy cockle salad.
Jane	:	(We) take one of each.

คำศัพท์ Vocabulary

Vocabulary	Definition	Note
 ไก่อบโอ่ง gài-òp-òhng	*Specific name* clay pot roasted chicken	
อบ òp	*Verb* 1. [to] bake, roast 2. [to] perfume, scent	
 โอ่ง òhng	*Noun* water jar, earthen jar	
 ไก่ผัดเม็ดมะม่วง gài-pàt- mét-má-mûuang	*Specific name* stir fried chicken with cashew nuts	
ผัด pàt	*Verb* 1. [to] fry 2. [to] postpone, delay, put off	
 เม็ดมะม่วง mét-má-mûuang	*Noun* cashew nut	Fun fact: 'เม็ด' (mét) by itself means 'seed' or 'grain' and 'มะม่วง' (má-mûuang) means 'mango'. A cashew nut is called 'เม็ดมะม่วง' (mét-má-mûuang) because it looks like a little seed/grain of the mangoes.

TSL4U

คำศัพท์ Vocabulary

Vocabulary	Definition	Note
 ไข่ยัดไส้ kài-yát-sâi	*Specific name* stuffed omelette	
ยัด yát	*Verb* [to] stuff, cram, squeeze	
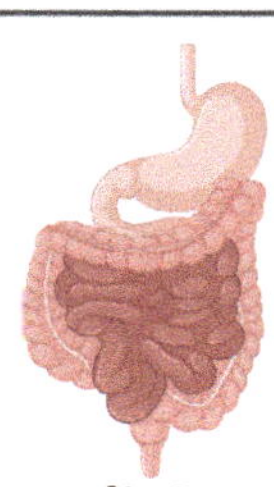 ไส้ sâi	*Noun* 1. intestine 2. the stuffing, filling, inside part	
 อาหารทะเล aa-hǎan-tá-lay	*Noun* seafood	
สิ sì	*Particle* We can't translate this meaning into a direct English equivalent. It's a particle used to show emphasis.	
น่ากิน nâa-gin	*Stative Verb; Adjective* [to be] tasty-looking, appetizing	

คำศัพท์ Vocabulary

Vocabulary	Definition	Note
แนะนำ náe-nam	*Verb* [to] introduce [to] advise, recommend	
เมนู may-noo	*Noun* menu	
 ปูผัดผงกะหรี่ bpoo-pàt-pŏng-gà-rèe	*Specific name* stir-fried crab with curry powder	
 ปู bpoo	*Noun* 1. crab *Verb* [to] cover, pave over	
 ผง pŏng	*Noun* powder, dirt, dust	
ผงกะหรี่ pŏng-gà-rèe	*Noun* curry powder	

คำศัพท์ Vocabulary

Vocabulary	Definition	Note
 ข้าวผัดสับปะรด kâao-pàt-sàp-bpà-rót	*Specific name* pineapple fried rice	
 สับปะรด sàp-bpà-rót	*Noun* pineapple	
 กุ้งราดซอสมะขาม gûng-râat-sót-má-kăam	*Specific name* crispy prawn in tamarind sauce	
 กุ้ง gûng	*Noun* shrimp, prawn, crayfish	
ราด râat	*Verb* [to] pour onto	
 ซอส sót	*Noun* sauce	
 มะขาม má-kăam	*Noun* tamarind	

คำศัพท์ Vocabulary

Vocabulary	Definition	Note
 **หมึกทอดกระเทียม** mèuk-tôt-grà-tiiam	*Specific name* crispy garlic calamari	
 **หมึก** mèuk	*Noun* 1. squid, calamari, octopus 2. ink	
ทอด tôt	*StativeVerb ; Adjective* 1. [to be] deep fried *Verb* 2. [to] fry 3. [to] extend, stretch out, cast out	
 **กระเทียม** grà-tiiam	*Noun* garlic	
 **ปลานึ่งมะนาว** bplaa-nêung-má-naao	*Specific name* steamed fish with lime	
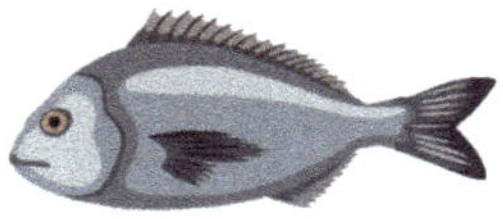 **ปลา** bplaa	*Noun* fish	

TSL4U

คำศัพท์ Vocabulary

Vocabulary	Definition	Note
นึ่ง nêung	*Verb* 1. [to] steam (food, cooking) *Stative Verb; Adjective* 2. [to be] steamed (food, cooking)	
 **มะนาว** má-naao	*Noun* lemon, lime	Fun fact: did you know that in Thailand we rarely use lemons in cooking, so we don't even have a word to for it. We use 'มะนาว' (má-naao) for both limes and lemons.
 **ยำหอยแครง** yam-hŏi-kraeng	*Specific name* spicy cockle salad	
ยำ yam	*Verb* 1. [to] mix, blend, mingle *Noun* 2. a type of Thai spicy salad	
 **หอยแครง** hŏi-kraeng	*Noun* cockle	
อย่างละหนึ่ง yàang-lá-nèung	*Combined words* one each	
ละ lá	*Quantifier* each, per, every	

Exercise 1 Listen to Thai sentences from your teacher and select the picture according to the sentence.

ฟังคุณครูพูดภาษาไทยและเลือกรูปภาพที่สอดคล้องกับประโยคที่คุณครูพูด

1. พอลอยากกินไก่ผัดเม็ดมะม่วง

2. เมนูแนะนำที่ร้านเป็นปูผัดผงกะหรี่

3. พอลไม่เคยกินยำหอยแครง

4. มาภูเก็ตต้องกินอาหารทะเล

A

B

C

5. อาหารทะเลมีกุ้ง หอย ปู ปลา

A

B

C

Exercise 2

Answer the questions below according to your situation.
ตอบคำถามต่อไปนี้ตามความเป็นจริง

1. คุณเคยไปภูเก็ตมั้ย Kun koiie bpai poo-gèt mái

....

2. คุณชอบอาหารทะเลอะไรมากที่สุด
Kun chôp aa-hăan-tá-lay à-rai mâak-têe-sùt

....

3. คุณเคยกินเมนูอะไรบ้าง Kun koiie gin may-noo à-rai bâang

....

4. ถ้าไปภูเก็ต คุณอยากกินอะไร Tâa bpai poo-gèt kun yàak gin à-rai

....

5. ทายซิ ทั้งหมดราคาเท่าไหร่ Taai-sí táng-mòt raa-kaa tâo-rài

....

Grammar 1

มาภูเก็ตก็ต้องกินอาหารทะเลสิ

Maa poo-gèt gôr-dtông-gin aa-hăan-tá-lay sì

Come to Phuket, (you) must eat seafood.

Structure: sentence + สิ (sì)

Explanation and Example:

สิ (sì) is a particle used to show emphasis of the verb in that particular sentence. It can convey 3 meanings/feelings depending on the content and context.

Meaning / Feeling	Example
1. Commanding	เดินเร็ว ๆ สิ (dern-reo-reo sì) Walk fast. เชื่อฉันสิ (chêuua-chăn sì) Believe me.
2. Inviting	ไปด้วยกันสิ (bpai-dûuay-gan sì) Let's go together. เข้ามาสิ (kâo-maa sì) Come in please.
3. Definitely yes (when answering yes-no question, an invitation or a request.)	ได้สิ (dâai sì) Surely can. เอาสิ (ao sì) Surely take (it).

You may hear ดิ (dì) in spoken language. It is the same as สิ (sì) but more casual.

Exercise 1 Read Thai sentences and translate them into English.
อ่านประโยคภาษาไทยและแปลเป็นภาษาอังกฤษ

1.) อยู่เมืองไทยก็ต้องพูดภาษาไทยสิ
Yòo-meuuang-tai gôr-dtông-pôot-paa-săa-tai sì

....

2.) คุณเรียนภาษาไทยสิ
Kun riian-paa-săa-tai sì

....

3.) คุณไม่พูดภาษาอังกฤษสิ
Kun mâi-pôot-paa-săa-ang-grìt sì

....

4.) พวกเราพูดภาษาไทยกันสิ
Pûuak-rao pôot-paa-săa-tai-gan sì

....

5.) เอาสิ พวกเราพูดภาษาไทยกัน
Ao-sì pûuak-rao pôot-paa-săa-tai-gan

....

Exercise 2 Say these sentences in Thai.
พูดประโยคต่อไปนี้เป็นภาษาไทย

1. If you like Thailand, buy a house here.
2. If money is not enough, don't go shopping.
3. You don't go eating in the restaurant please.
4. Let's not go travelling too.
5. Surely can.

Grammar 2

น้องช่วยแนะนำหน่อย

Nóng chûuay-náe-nam nòi

Young brother, you help recommending please.

Structure: sentence + หน่อย (nòi)

Explanation:

'หน่อย' (nòi) as an adverb means 'a little, a bit'. For example, ผมพูดไทยได้นิดหน่อย (pŏm pôot-tai dâai-nít-nòi) I can speak Thai a little bit.

'หน่อย' (nòi) can also be a particle word, used to soften a request or command. It can be indirectly translated as 'please' like in the sentence above. น้องช่วยแนะนำหน่อย (nóng chûuay-náe-nam nòi) Young brother, you help recommending please.

Example:

1. ขอลองเสื้อตัวนี้หน่อย
   Kŏr-long sêuua-dtuua-née nòi
   Can (I) please try this shirt?

2. เสื้อตัวนี้ใหญ่ไปหน่อย ใส่ไม่พอดี
   Sêuua-dtuua-née yài-bpai-nòi sài-mâi-por-dee
   This shirt is a little bit too big, doesn't fit (me).

3. ราคาก็แพงเกินไปหน่อย
   Raa-kaa gôr paeng-gern-bpai nòi
   The price is also a little bit too expensive.

4. ลดราคาหน่อยได้มั้ย
   Lót-raa-kaa nòi dâai-mái
   Can (you) please reduce the price?

5. ลดได้นิดหน่อยถ้าจ่ายเงินสด
   Lót-dâai-nít-nòi tâa-jàai-ngern-sòt
   (I) can reduce the price a little bit, if (you) pay cash.

Exercise 1

Read Thai sentences and translate them into English.
อ่านประโยคภาษาไทยและแปลเป็นภาษาอังกฤษ

1.) ฉันอ้วนขึ้นนิดหน่อย
Chăn ûuan-kêun nít-nòi

....

2.) คุณออกกำลังกายเป็นเพื่อนฉันหน่อยได้มั้ย
Kun òk-gam-lang-gaai bpen-pêuuan-chăn nòi dâai-mái

....

3.) ได้สิ ฉันก็อยากลดความอ้วนหน่อยเหมือนกัน
Dâai-sì chăn-gôr-yàak lót-kwaam-ûuan nòi mĕuuan-gan

....

4.) ออกกำลังกาย แล้วก็กินข้าวเย็นนิดหน่อย
Òk-gam-lang-gaai láew-gôr gin-kâao-yen nít-nòi

....

5.) พวกเราต้องทำได้ สู้ ๆ หน่อย
Pûuak-rao dtông-tam-dâai sôo-sôo-nòi

....

Exercise 2

Say these sentences in Thai.
พูดประโยคต่อไปนี้เป็นภาษาไทย

1. Wait for me please.
2. Walk slowly please.
3. I am a little bit tired.
4. Can I have water please?
5. Put a little bit of ice too.

Grammar 3

เอามาอย่างละ 1

Ao-maa yàang-lá-nèung

Take one of each.

Structure and Explanation:

'ละ' (lá) is a quantifier similar to 'each, per, every' in English; however in Thai language, the structure is as following:

classifier + ละ (lá) + number

Example:

1. ผมออกกำลังกายอาทิตย์ละ 3 ครั้ง
   Pŏm òk-gam-lang-gaai aa-tít-lá săam-kráng
   I exercise 3 times per week.

2. ผมว่ายน้ำครั้งละ 30 นาที
   Pŏm wâai-náam kráng-lá săam-sìp-naa-tee
   I swim 30 minutes each time.

3. ผมวิ่งได้ชั่วโมงละ 7 กิโล
   Pŏm wîng-dâai chûua-mohng-lá jèt-gì-loh
   I can run 7 kilometers per hour.

4. ผมยกน้ำหนักได้ครั้งละ 10 กิโล
   Pŏm yók-náam-nàk-dâai kráng-lá sìp-gì-loh
   I can lift weight 10 kilograms each time.

5. แล้วคุณล่ะ ออกกำลังกายวันละกี่นาที
   Láew-kun-lâ òk-gam-lang-gaai wan-lá gèe-naa-tee
   What about you? How many minutes do you exercise per day?

Note: 'percent' is an English loanword which widely used in Thai language. The Thai word for 'percentage' is ร้อยละ (rói-lá) – which can be directly translated as 'per hundred'. For example:

6. ปี 2020 ดอกเบี้ยบ้านแค่ร้อยละ 3 เอง
   Bpee sŏng-pan-yêe-sìp dòk-bîia-bâan kâe rói-lá săam eng)
   In 2020, the home interest rate was only 3 percent.

Exercise 1 Read Thai sentences and translate them into English.
อ่านประโยคภาษาไทยและแปลเป็นภาษาอังกฤษ

1.) เสื้อตัวละ 350 บาท
Sêuua dtuua-lá săam-rói-hâa-sìp-bàat

....

2.) กางเกงตัวละ 490 บาท
Gaang-geng dtuua-lá sèe-rói-gâo-sìp-bàat

....

3.) รองเท้าคู่ละ 2,200 บาท
Rong-táo kôo-lá sŏng-pan-sŏng-rói-bàat

....

4.) หมวกใบละ 180 บาท
Mùuak bai-lá nèung-rói-bpàet-sìp-bàat

....

5.) แว่นตาอันละกี่บาท
Wâen-dtaa an-lá gèe-bàat

....

Exercise 2 Say these sentences in Thai.
พูดประโยคต่อไปนี้เป็นภาษาไทย

1. Noodle is 60 Baht per bowl.
2. Cake is 95 Baht per piece.
3. Mangoes are 110 Baht per kilogram.
4. Hainanese chicken rice, how much is it per plate?
5. Smoothie, how many baht is it per glass?

Fun Fact:

In Thailand, when you go out to eat with friends or family, it's common to order lots of different dishes and share them with everyone at the table. Instead of each person getting their own meal, you all choose a mix of dishes, which are then put in the middle of the table for everyone to try. This way, you get to taste a variety of flavors and enjoy different types of food together. It makes the meal more fun and brings everyone closer together.

Challenge: List as many Thai dishes as you know.

Chapter 12

ผมยังโสด

Pŏm-yang-sòht

I am still single.

พอลคุยโทรศัพท์กับแสนดี Paul kui-toh-rá-sàp gàp Săen-dee

โปรดติดตามตอนต่อไป

Bpròht-dtìt-dtaam-dton-dtòr-bpai

English Translation

Paul talks to San-dee on the phone.

San-dee : (You) have been to Phuket with the office, how has it been?

Paul : I really like it. The sea in Thailand is very beautiful. The seafood is also fresh. The service at the accommodation is good. I also got upgraded to a better room.

San-dee : The mountains in Thailand are beautiful as well. If you like, try inviting your friends to go to Chiang Mai and see (how it goes).

Paul : I (will) try asking (my) friends and see (how it goes).
(I am) not sure, whom will be able to go?
At this time, I see everyone is busy with work.

Paul : If I have a partner, it would be good.
So that (I) can go with (my) partner.

San-dee : Don't you have a partner yet?

Paul : No, I'm still single.

San-dee : ....

Paul : San-dee, are you still there?

San-dee : Yes, I am.
I am also still single.

To be continued.

TSL4U

คำศัพท์ Vocabulary

Vocabulary	Definition	Note
 **คุย** kui	*Verb* [to] talk, chat, speak	
 **โทรศัพท์** toh-rá-sàp	*Noun* telephone, phone	
ที่ทำงาน têe-tam-ngaan	*Noun* workplace, office	
ที่พัก têe-pák	*Noun* residence, home, accommodation	
 **ภูเขา** poo-kăo	*Noun* hill, mountain	
ชวน chuuan	*Verb* 1. [to] persuade, induce 2. [to] invite	

คำศัพท์ Vocabulary

Vocabulary	Definition	Note
เชียงใหม่ chiiang-mài	*Specific name* Chiang Mai	
เดี๋ยว dǐieow	*Noun* 1. moment *Adverb* 2. in just a minute, in just a moment	Fun Fact: although 'เดี๋ยว' (dǐieow) literally means 'in a moment'; sometimes 'a moment' for Thai people can be very long. When Paul said "เดี๋ยวถามเพื่อน ๆ" (dǐieow-tǎam-pêuuan-pêuuan); he doesn't mean he will ask his friends in a moment. He actually means "I will ask my friends later (not now).
แน่ใจ nâe-jai	*Verb* [to] be sure, be confident, be certain	
ไม่แน่ใจ mâi-nâe-jai	*Combined words* not sure	
ช่วงนี้ chûuang-née	*Adverb* at this period, at this time	
ช่วง chûuang	*Noun* period, section, part	
ทุกคน túk-kon	*Indefinite Pronoun* everyone, everybody	

คำศัพท์ Vocabulary

Vocabulary	Definition	Note
น่าจะ nâa-jà	*AdverbAuxiliary* should, had better likely	
โสด sòht	*StativeVerb ; Adjective* [to be] single, unmarried	
ยังโสด yang-sòht	*Combined words* still single	
โปรด bpròht	*Adverb Auxiliary* 1. please *Stative Verb* 2. [to be] favorite *Verb* 3. [to] help, assist, aid	
ติดตาม dtit-dtaam	*Verb* 1. [to] follow, be in company with, accompany 2. [to] pay attention, take note of, concern	
ต่อไป dtòr-bpai	*Adverb* 1. continually, further, afterward 2. next, latter, later	

Phrase

Phrase	Definition	Note
เป็นยังไงบ้าง bpen-yang-ngai-bâang	1. How is it going? 2. How are you doing?	
ขอคิดดูก่อน kŏr-kít-doo-gòn	Let me think about it.	
ลอง........... ดูสิ long .... doo-sì	Try .... and see.	
.... ก็น่าจะดี ....gôr-nâa-jà-dee	.... should be good.	
โปรดติดตามตอนต่อไป bpròht-dtìt-dtaam-dton-dtòr-bpai	To be continued.	

Exercise 1 Choose the correct answer.
เลือกคำตอบที่ถูกต้อง

1. พอลชอบภูเก็ตเพราะอะไร
(Paul chôp poo-gèt prór à-rai)

a ทะเลสวย (Tá-lay sŭuay)

b อาหารทะเลสด (Aa-hăan-tá-lay sòt)

c ทั้งสองอย่าง (Táng-sŏng-yàang)

2. ถ้าชอบภูเขา ต้องไปที่ไหน
(Tâa chôp poo-kăo dtông-bpai-têe-năi)

a พัทยา (Pát-tá-yaa)

b กรุงเทพ (Grung-têp)

c เชียงใหม่ (Chiiang-mài)

3. คนโสดคือคนแบบไหน
(Kon-sòht keu kon-bàep-năi)

a คนไม่มีแฟน (Kon mâi-mee faen)

b คนไม่มีเพื่อน (Kon mâi-mee pêuuan)

c คนไม่มีเงิน (Kon mâi-mee ngern)

4. ใครยังไม่มีแฟน
(Krai yang-mâi-mee faen)

a พอล (Paul)

b แสนดี (Săen-dee)

c ทั้งสองคน (Táng-sŏng-kon)

5. คุณคิดว่าพวกเขาจะเป็นแฟนกันมั้ย
(Kun kít-wâa pûuak-kăo jà bpen-faen-gan-mái)

a เป็น (Bpen)

b ไม่เป็น (Mâi-bpen)

c ไม่รู้ (Mâi-róo)

Exercise 2

Review chapter 1-12 and complete sentences with correct words.
ทบทวนบทที่ 1-12 และเติมคำในช่องว่างด้วยคำที่ถูกต้อง

ร้านอาหารตามสั่ง ráan-aa-hăan-dtaam-sàng	วัน wan	จอง jong	เมนู may-noo	แฟน faen	ยุ่ง yûng
นิดหน่อย nít-nòi	ทำอะไร tam-à-rai	ประเทศไทย bprà-têt-tai	ยังไง yang-ngai	ตัว dtuua	ชาบู chaa-boo

1. ยินดีต้อนรับสู่ ....
Yin-dee-dtôn-ráp-sòo........................

2. ไปอโศก...
Bpai à-sòhk ....

3. ผมพูดไทยได้....................................
Pŏm pôot-tai dâai ....

4. เสาร์อาทิตย์นี้....................................
Săo-aa-tít-née ....

5. พอลกับแสนดีไปกิน .... ด้วยกัน
Paul gàp Săen-dee bpai gin ....
dûuay gan

6. วันนี้คุณ .... มั้ย
Wan-née kun .... mái

7. บ้านพอลที่ออสเตรเลียมีโกลเด้น 1 ....
Bâan Paul têe Australia mee
gol-dên nèung............................

8. .... มีอาหารให้เลือกหลายอย่าง
.... mee aa-hăan hâi-lêuuak
lăai-yàang

9. ผมขอจองรถ 4 ....
Pŏm kŏr jong-rót sèe.............................

10. ผมขอ .... ห้อง 3 คืน
Pŏm kŏr .... hông săam-keun

11. ร้านอาหารมี .... อะไรแนะนำบ้าง
Ráan-aa-hăan mee .... à-rai
náe-nam bâang

12. เหงาจังเลย อยากมี .... แล้ว
Ngăo-jang-loiie Yàak mee .... láew

Grammar 1

ไปภูเก็ตกับที่ทำงานมา

Bpai-poo-gèt gàp-têe-tam-ngaan maa

Have been to Phuket with the office.

Structure:

1. 'มา' (maa) as a main verb meaning 'to come, arrive'. For example, ฉันมาประเทศไทย (chăn-maa-bprà-têt-tai) I come to Thailand.

2. 'มา' (maa) at the end of sentence can also act as a 'time indicator' for 'past tense' or 'present perfect tense'. For example, ไปภูเก็ตมา (bpai poo-gèt maa) Have been to Phuket. For review, please revisit grammar 1 in chapter 3.

3. The last function of มา (maa) is as a secondary verb meaning 'to, into, towards'. For example, ผมขับรถมาทำงาน (pŏm kàp-rót maa-tam-ngaan) I drive to work. (I am at work at the time of saying.)

Example:

1. ผมเคยมาที่นี่
   Pŏm koiie-maa têe-nêe
   I have come here.

2. คุณจะมาเมื่อไหร่
   Kun jà-maa mêuua-rài
   When will you come?

3. คุณไปที่ไหนมา
   Kun bpai-têe-năi maa
   Where have you gone?
   (Where have you been?)

4. ฉันไปวิ่งมา
   Chăn bpai-wîng maa
   I went running.

5. คุณออกมาข้างนอกได้มั้ย
   Kun òk-maa kâang-nôk dâai-mái
   Can you get (to) outside?

6. คุณเข้ามาข้างในได้เลย
   Kun kâo-maa kâang-nai dâai-loiie
   You can get (to) inside.

Additional note:

Similar to 'มา' (maa); 'ไป' (bpai) also can be used in 3 contexts:

1. As a main verb meaning ' (to) go, leave, depart'. For example, ฉันไปประเทศไทย (chăn-bpai-bprà-têt-tai) I go to Thailand.

2. As a secondary verb meanings 'to, away, into'. For example, ผมขับรถไปทำงาน (pŏm kàp-rót bpai-tam-ngaan) I drive to work. 'ไป' (bpai) in this sentence emphasises that when I go 'to' work, I drive.

3. At the end of sentence, as a 'time indicator' for 'past tense' or 'present perfect tense' – involving something that has disappeared or is no longer present. For example: ไม่มีไอติม น้องกินไปแล้ว (Mâi-mee-ai-dtim nóng-gin-bpai-láew) There is no ice-cream, younger brother/sister has eaten (it) already. (So the ice-cream has gone / no more ice-cream.)

Exercise 1

Read Thai sentences and translate them into English.
อ่านประโยคภาษาไทยและแปลเป็นภาษาอังกฤษ

1.) ขอโทษครับ ผมมาช้า
Kŏr-tôht-kráp pŏm-maa-cháa

....

2.) ผมไม่เคยมาที่นี่
Pŏm mâi-koiie-maa têe-nêe

....

3.) คุณโทรมาเหรอ
Kun toh-maa rĕr

....

4.) ใช่ครับ ผมโทรไปเอง
Châi-kráp pŏm toh-bpai eng

....

5.) คุณกินอะไรมาหรือยัง
Kun gin-à-rai maa rĕu-yang

....

6.) ผมกินคุกกี้ไป 2 ชิ้น แล้วคุณล่ะ
Pŏm gin cookie bpai-sŏng-chín láew-kun-lâ

....

Exercise 2

Say these sentences in Thai.
พูดประโยคต่อไปนี้เป็นภาษาไทย

1. Whom do you come with?
2. I come with my brother.
3. We drive a car to here.
4. Where do they walk to?
5. Have they eaten anything yet?
6. They had 2 pieces of pizza.

Grammar 2

ใครจะไปได้บ้าง
Krai jà-bpai dâai-bâang
Whom will be able to go?

Structure: (subject +) จะ jà + verb (+ object or extension)

Explanation:

'จะ' (jà) is an adverb auxiliary meaning 'will, shall'. It is put in front of a verb as per structure above, to form 'future tense' sentences.
For negative sentences, it follows structure below:

subject + จะ jà + ไม่ mâi + verb (+ object or extension)

Example:

1. พรุ่งนี้เขาจะไม่ทำงาน
Prûng-née kǎo jà-mâi-tam-ngaan
Tomorrow he will not work.

2. พวกเราจะไปเชียงใหม่ด้วยกัน
Pûuak-rao jà-bpai chiiang-mài dûuay-gan
We will go to Chiangmai together.

3. ใครจะจองโรงแรม
Krai jà-jong rohng-raem
Who will book the hotel?

4. (พวกเรา) จะออกจากที่นี่เมื่อไหร่
(Pûuak-rao) Jà-òk-jàak têe-nêe mêuua-rài
When will (we) leave from here?

5. (พวกเรา) จะอยู่ที่นั่นกี่วัน
(Pûuak-rao) Jà-yòo têe-nân gèe-wan
How many days will (we) stay there?

Exercise 1

Read Thai sentences and translate them into English.
อ่านประโยคภาษาไทยและแปลเป็นภาษาอังกฤษ

1.) พวกเราจะนั่งเครื่องบินไปเชียงใหม่
Pûuak-rao jà-nâng-krêuuang-bin bpai-chiiang-mài

2.) คุณจะมารับพวกเราได้มั้ย
Kun jà-maa-ráp pûuak-rao dâai-mái

3.) คุณจะมาถึงกี่โมง
Kun jà-maa-tĕung gèe-mohng

4.) พวกเราจะเช่ารถดีมั้ย
Pûuak-rao jà-châo-rót dee-mái

5.) ใครจะขับรถให้พวกเรา
Krai jà-kàp-rót hâi-pûuak-rao

Exercise 2

Say these sentences in Thai.
พูดประโยคต่อไปนี้เป็นภาษาไทย

1. What will you eat this evening?
2. We will eat Jimjum (Thai-style hot pot).
3. How will you go to the restaurant?
4. We will walk to there.
5. What time will the restaurant open?
6. I don't know. I will call to ask.

Additional note 1:

Although 'จะ' (jà) is equivalent to 'will' in English – which make sentences 'future tenses'; in Thai we can omit the word จะ (jà) and still form 'future tenses' if the context is talking about the future; or there is another 'time indicator' word.

For example:

Translation	Future Sentence with จะ jà	Future Sentence without จะ jà
Where will (you) go?	จะไปไหน Jà bpai năi	ไปไหน Bpai-năi ** the context is asking someone who is about to go somewhere.*
Tomorrow, will you come to work?	พรุ่งนี้คุณจะมาทำงานมั้ย Prûng-née kun jà-maa-tam-ngaan mái	พรุ่งนี้คุณมาทำงานมั้ย Prûng-née kun maa-tam-ngaan mái ** time indicator is the word 'tomorrow'.*
What time will he come here?	เขาจะมาที่นี่กี่โมง Kăo jà-maa têe-nêe gèe-mohng	เขามาที่นี่กี่โมง Kăo maa têe-nêe gèe-mohng **the context is that he is not here at present, so what time will he come in the future.*

Additional note 2:

ถ้าผมมีแฟน จะได้ไปกับแฟน
Tâa-pŏm-mee-faen jà-dâai-bpai-gàp-faen
If I have a partner, so that I can go with (my) partner.

Explanation:

'จะได้' (jà-dâai) is a combined word meaning 'so that'. It is used in the situation that, only if For example, ถ้าผมมีแฟน ผมจะได้ไปกับแฟน (Tâa-pŏm-mee-faen pŏm-jà-dâai-bpai-gàp-faen) Only if I have a partner, I can go with (my) partner.

Structure: condition (+ subject) + จะได้ (jà-dâai) + verb

For example:

1. กินข้าว จะได้กินยา
Gin-kâao jà-dâai gin-yaa
Eat, so that (you) will be able to eat medicine.

2. ทำงานดี ๆ จะได้มีโบนัส
Tam-ngaan-dee-dee jà-dâai mee bonus
Work well, so that (we) will get bonus.

3. ถ้าวันนี้ฝนตก ฉันจะได้ไม่ซักผ้า
Tâa-wan-née-fŏn-dtòk chăn-jà-dâai mâi-sák-pâa
If today rains, so that I will not wash clothes.

4. ถ้าคุณไม่ไปด้วยกัน ฉันจะได้ไปเอง
Tâa-kun-mâi-bpai-dûuay-gan chăn-jà-dâai bpai eng
If you don't go together, so that I will go myself.

5. ลดราคาให้หน่อย จะได้มาซื้อบ่อย ๆ
Lót-raa-kaa-hâi-nòi jà-dâai maa-séu-bòi-bòi
Please discount a bit, so that (I) will come to buy often.

Grammar 3

ผมลองถามเพื่อน ๆ ดู

Pǒm long-tǎam pêuuan-pêuuan-doo

I try asking my friends and see (how it goes).

Structure and Explanation:

ลองดู (long-doo) literally means 'try and see how it goes'.

Note 1: 'ลอง' (long) means 'to try' as to check it out, to find out about something or someone.

Note 2: If you are 'to try' as 'to attempt' or to put an effort into doing something; in Thai we use the word 'พยายาม' (pá-yaa-yaam).

1. 'ลองดู' (long-doo) can be used together to simply convince someone to 'try and see how it goes'.

For example, ขับรถในประเทศไทยไม่ยาก ลองดูสิ (kàp-rót nai-bprà-têt-tai mâi-yâak long-doo-sì) Driving in Thailand is not difficult, try and see how it goes.

2. Alternatively, we can add more details (verb and extension) between 'ลอง' (long) and 'ดู' (doo). In this case, the structure will look like: ลอง (long) + verb (+ extension)+ ดู (doo) but still have the same meaning as 'try and see how it goes'.

For example, ขับรถในประเทศไทยไม่ยาก ลองขับดูสิ (kàp-rót nai-bprà-têt-tai mâi-yâak long-kàp-doo-sì) Driving in Thailand is not difficult, try driving and see how it goes.

Example:

1. อันนี้อร่อย ลองกินดูสิ
An-née à-ròi long-gin-doo-sì
This one is delicious, try eating and see.

2. เพลงนี้เพราะมาก ลองฟังดูนะ
Pleng-née prór-mâak long-fang-doo-ná
This song sounds very good, try listening and see.

3. มีห้างเปิดใหม่ ลองไปดูมั้ย
Mee-hâang bpèrt-mài long-bpai-doo-mái
There is a new shopping center opening,
(do you want to) try visiting and see?

4. คุณไม่เคยกินส้มตำเหรอ ลองดูสิ
Kun mâi-koiie-gin sôm-dtam rěr long-doo-sì
Have you never tried Somtum? Try and see.

5. เกมนี้สนุกนะ ลองดูมั้ย
Geme-née-sà-nùk-ná long-doo-mái
This game is fun, (do you want to) try and see?

Exercise 1

Read Thai sentences and translate them into English.
อ่านประโยคภาษาไทยและแปลเป็นภาษาอังกฤษ

1.) อยากลองดูมั้ย
Yàak long-doo-mái

....

2.) เคยลองดูรึยัง
Koiie long-doo réu-yang

....

3.) ลองดูอีกครั้ง
Long-doo èek-kráng

....

4.) ลองดูใหม่
Long-doo mài

....

5.) ลองดูก่อน
Long-doo gòn

....

Exercise 2

Say these sentences in Thai.
พูดประโยคต่อไปนี้เป็นภาษาไทย

1. Chatuchak market has everything, try going and see.
2. This plate of Somtum is really not spicy, try eating and see.
3. The dog is over there, do you want to try going and see?
4. These pants are nice, let's try and see.
5. Did you not see the plants? Let's and see one more time.

Fun fact:

1. In Thailand, the most popular communication is LINE. Thai people use LINE app for all types of communication- from personal, work to business purposes.

2. Many large businesses send promotional content to their LINE subscribers instead of email list. Some companies even integrated LINE shop and LINE pay into their operations.

3. Stickers and emojis are commonly used in Thai digital communications. These expressive icons are used to convey emotions, messages, and humor in chats, making LINE stickers an iconic element of Thailand digital culture.

4. The popularity of these stickers has created a side business. Many Thai artists design and sell custom sticker packs. Some artists have become millionaires from selling LINE stickers.

Challenge: Can you guess what will happen in the next book? Discuss in Thai if you can.

Curriculum Developers

CURRICULUM DEVELOPER

THORAPORN THOWRUNGRUANG
(TARA THOW)
ธรพร ไถวรุงเรือง (แอดมินตุล)

About

- Originally from Songkhla, received education until 10th grade at Alexander's International School in the UK and completed high school at Christchurch Girls' High School in New Zealand.
- Earned Bachelor of Economics and Social Science from University of Sydney.
- Completed Master of Business Administration (MBA) from University of Technology, Sydney (UTS) in Australia.
- A mother of two children, a boy and a girl, residing in Sydney, with a strong desire for her kids to be fluent in Thai.
- Former co-owner of Thai Kids Academy and Co-founder of TSLTK (Thai as - Second Language by Thai Kids Academy)
- Interested in personal development, meditation, reading, writing, singing, Chinese and BL series.

- เกิดและโตที่จังหวัดสงขลา เรียนถึง Year 10 ที่ Alexanders International School ประเทศอังกฤษ และจบมัธยมปลายจาก Christchurch Girls' High School ประเทศนิวซีแลนด์
- จบปริญญาตรีสาขาเศรษฐศาสตร์และสังคมศาสตร์จาก The University of Sydney และปริญญาโทสาขาบริหารธุรกิจจาก The University of Technology, Sydney (UTS) ประเทศออสเตรเลีย
- อาศัยอยู่ที่ซิดนีย์ เป็นคุณแม่ของลูก ๆ ที่น่ารักสองคน (ชายหนึ่ง หญิงหนึ่ง) และอยากให้ลูก ๆ สามารถพูดภาษาไทยได้
- อดีตหุ้นส่วน Thai Kids Academy และร่วมก่อตั้ง TSLTK (Thai as Second Language by Thai Kids Academy)
- สนใจศาสตร์พัฒนาตัวเอง ทำสมาธิ อ่านหนังสือ เขียนหนังสือ ร้องเพลง ภาษาจีน และซีรีส์วาย

JEERAPA DEERAKSA (KRU NERY / DEMI)
จีระภา ดีรักษา (ครูเนย/เดมี)

About

- Graduated with a Bachelor of Education, Major in Social Studies from Chiangmai University, achieving First Class Honours.
- Enjoys delving into a diverse range of interests, including reading books on culture, way of life, society, history, cooking, and photography, and sharing intriguing and amusing stories with students.
- Started teaching as a freshman and has a passion for education, opening a YouTube channel and Facebook page "Demi 1 Learn Thai" to share Thai language skills, teaching tips, and lifestyle experiences with students from all over the world.
- Led an active lifestyle since high school, participating in camps and academic competitions, and embarking on field trips for personal growth, cultural enrichment, and travel experiences. Visited 48 provinces in Thailand during my student years and recently gained exposure to six countries in ASEAN.
- Working as an online Thai teacher for non-native speakers and recently concluded a two-year au pair program in New York, USA.

- จบปริญญาตรีจากคณะศึกษาศาสตร์ มหาวิทยาลัยเชียงใหม่ วิชาเอกสังคมศึกษา (เกียรตินิยมอันดับ1)
- ชอบอ่านหนังสือ สนใจในเรื่องวัฒนธรรม วิถีชีวิต สังคม ประวัติศาสตร์ ทำอาหาร ถ่ายภาพ สนุกกับการที่ได้เล่าเรื่องราวแปลก ๆ สนุกสนานที่ได้ค้นพบและนำมาแบ่งปันให้กับนักเรียน
- เริ่มต้นการสอนตั้งแต่เป็นนักศึกษา ปี 1 สนุกกับงานสอนเสมอ เปิดช่อง YouTube และ Facebook page ชื่อ Demi 1 learn Thai สำหรับสอนภาษาไทยให้ชาวต่างชาติ แชร์ทักษะภาษาไทย ทักษะการสอน และการใช้ชีวิตกับนักเรียนจากทั่วทุกมุมโลก
- เป็นเด็กกิจกรรมมาโดยตลอดตั้งแต่สมัยเรียนมัธยม จนเรียนจบมหาวิทยาลัย เข้าค่าย แข่งขันด้านวิชาการ เข้าร่วมการจัดทัศนศึกษา โดยมีเป้าหมายเพื่อเก็บเกี่ยวประสบการณ์ ความรู้รอบตัว และท่องเที่ยว จบ ป.ตรี ด้วยการท่องเที่ยวในไทยมากกว่า 48 จังหวัด และล่าสุดได้มีโอกาสเดินทางไป 6 ประเทศในอาเซียน
- ปัจจุบันเป็นครูสอนภาษาไทยออนไลน์ให้ชาวต่างชาติ และเข้าร่วมโครงการออแพร์ ที่นิวยอร์ก สหรัฐอเมริกา เป็นเวลา 2 ปี

SUTEEMA SRISUM-ANG
(KRU PREM)
สุธีมา ศรีสำอางค์ (ครูเปรม)

About

- Earned a Bachelor of Science in Logistics Management from the Faculty of Logistics at Burapha University and a Master of Business Administration from Stamford International University.
- Passionate about teaching and interested in psychology, particularly in children, families, and teaching. Started teaching Math and English as a tutor right after high school.
- Has been teaching Thai to foreigners since 2020. Finds this work fulfilling and has a deep appreciation for the value of teaching Thai as a second language, as it helps mixed children communicate with their families and allows foreigners from various countries to understand Thai language and culture.
- Continuously strives to learn and improve in teaching Thai as a second language, drawing from theories of Thai language and teaching, as well as the experiences gained from each student. Became involved with TSLTK by Thai Kids Academy and participated in their 5th generation teaching training course, leading to a current role as a teacher at Thai Kids Academy.

- จบปริญญาตรีวิทยาศาสตร์บัณฑิต การจัดการโลจิสติกส์ มหาวิทยาลัยบูรพา และปริญญาโท บริหารธุรกิจมหาบัณฑิต มหาวิทยาลัยนานาชาติแสตมฟอร์ด
- รักในงานสอน และสนใจในด้านจิตวิทยาโดยเฉพาะในเด็ก ครอบครัว และการสอน เริ่มงานด้านการสอนจากการเป็นติวเตอร์คณิตศาสตร์และภาษาอังกฤษตั้งแต่จบมัธยมปลาย
- เริ่มสอนภาษาไทยให้ชาวต่างชาติ เมื่อปี พ.ศ. 2563 หลงใหลและมีความสุขในโลกของการสอนภาษาไทยให้ชาวต่างชาติและตระหนักในคุณค่าของการสอน มีความสุขที่เห็นเด็ก ๆ ลูกครึ่งสื่อสารและอ่าน-เขียนภาษาไทยได้ รวมถึงชาวต่างชาติต่างภาษาที่รักในภาษาไทยและความเป็นไทยของเราได้เรียนรู้และเข้าใจภาษาและวัฒนธรรม
- ตั้งใจเรียนรู้ และพัฒนาตนเองอย่างต่อเนื่องในด้านการสอนภาษาไทยทั้งจากทฤษฎี หลักไวยากรณ์ของภาษา และจากประสบการณ์การสอนนักเรียนทุก ๆ คน จนได้มาพบกับหลักสูตร TSLTK by Thai Kids Academy และเข้าอบรมรุ่นที่ 5 จนมาสู่การได้ร่วมงานและเป็นหนึ่งในทีมคุณครูของ Thai Kids Academy ในปัจจุบัน

HATAICHANOK KERDKAMBOT
(KRU OH)
หทัยชนก เกิดกำบท (ครูโอะ)

About

- Holds Bachelor of Arts, in Journalism and Mass Communication, Thammasat University.
- Former Administrative Assistant of the Vice President of Supply Chain, Triumph Aviation Group Inc. (THAILAND).
- Currently works as a trainer at New Counseling Service and teaches English to non-native speakers, as well as teaching Thai to foreigners.
- Has a strong interest to promote and engage in social justice, equality in income, opportunities and rights, and holistic health and wellness, and actively volunteers in related causes.

- จบปริญญาตรีจากคณะวารสารศาสตร์ มหาวิทยาลัยธรรมศาสตร์
- อดีตผู้ช่วยผู้บริหาร Triumph Aviation Group Inc. (THAILAND)
- ปัจจุบันเป็นวิทยากรบริษัท New Counseling Service และครูสอนภาษาอังกฤษ และครูสอนภาษาไทยให้ชาวต่างชาติ
- สนใจและส่งเสริมด้าน Holistic Health การมีสุขภาวะที่ดีแบบองค์รวม ความยุติธรรม และความเท่าเทียมกันในสังคม ทั้งด้านสิทธิ โอกาส และรายได้

www.ingramcontent.com/pod-product-compliance
Lightning Source LLC
Chambersburg PA
CBHW041512210926
51847CB00011B/121
* 9 7 8 6 1 6 6 1 9 2 0 9 4 *